CityPack
Washington

**MARY CASE
AND
BRUCE WALKER**

*Mary Case has lived on
Capitol Hill in Washington DC
since being appointed manager
of the Smithsonian Institution's
140 million objects and
specimens in 1986. Currently
she is a travel writer and
consultant in management
issues to the non-profit arts and
cultural community.*

*Bruce Walker works on the
weekend section of* The
Washington Post. *He explores
the city on bike and
particularly enjoys the diversity
of restaurants and nightlife
Washington has to offer.*

AA Publishing

Page 1: *Stars and Stripes and the US Capitol*

Page 2: *Georgetown stores*

Page 13 (a): *US Marine Corps Memorial*
Page 13 (b): *The Capitol dome*

Page 28: *Vietnam Veterans Memorial*

Page 49 (a): *Washington cherry blossoms*
Page 49 (b): *Capital Children's Museum*

Page 87 (a): *The Metro*
Page 87 (b): *Old Town Trolleybus*

Written by Mary Case and Bruce Walker (restaurants, hotels and Travel Facts)
Edited, designed and produced by AA Publishing
Maps © The Automobile Association 1996
Fold-out map:
  © RV Reise- und Verkehrsverlag Munich · Stuttgart
  © Cartography: GeoData

Distributed in the United Kingdom by AA Publishing, Norfolk House, Priestley Road, Basingstoke, Hampshire, RG24 9NY.

The contents of this publication are believed correct at the time of printing. Nevertheless, the publishers cannot be held responsible for any errors or omissions or for changes in the details given in this guide or for the consequences of any reliance on the information provided by the same. Assessments of attractions, hotels, restaurants and so forth are based upon the author's own personal experience and, therefore, descriptions given in this guide necessarily contain an element of subjective opinion which may not reflect the publishers' opinion or dictate a reader's own experiences on another occasion.

We have tried to ensure accuracy in this guide, but things do change and we would be grateful if readers would advise us of any inaccuracies they may encounter.

A CIP catalogue record for this book is available from the British Library.
ISBN 0 7495 1185 0

Published by AA Publishing (a trading name of Automobile Association Developments Limited, whose registered office is Norfolk House, Priestley Road, Basingstoke, Hampshire RG24 9NY. Registered number 1878835).
Origination by BTB Colour Reproduction Ltd, Whitchurch, Hampshire
Printed and bound by Dai Nippon Printing Co. (Hong Kong) Ltd

Contents

About this book

CityPack Washington is divided into six sections to cover the six most important aspects of your visit to Washington.

1. WASHINGTON LIFE
(pages 5–12)
Your personal introduction to Washington by author Mary Case
  Facts and figures
  Leading characters
  Big events from Washington's history

2. HOW TO ORGANISE YOUR TIME *(pages 13–22)*
Make the most of your time in Washington
  4 one-day itineraries
  2 suggested walks
  2 evening strolls
  4 excursions beyond the city

3. WASHINGTON'S TOP 25 SIGHTS *(pages 23–48)*
Your concise guide to sightseeing
  Mary Case's own choice, with her personal introduction to each sight
  Description and history
  Highlights of each attraction
  Practical information

4. WASHINGTON'S BEST
(pages 49–60)
What Washington is renowned for
  African American Sites
  For Children
  Libraries & Archives
  Outdoor Spaces
  Places to Worship
  Views
  Practical details throughout

5. WASHINGTON: WHERE TO... *(pages 61–86)*
The best places to eat, shop, be entertained, and stay
  13 categories of restaurant
  13 categories of store
  6 categories of entertainment spot
  3 categories of hotel
  Price bands and booking details

6. WASHINGTON TRAVEL FACTS *(pages 87–93)*
Essential information for your stay

SYMBOLS
Throughout the guide a few straightforward symbols are used to denote the following categories:

✚ map reference on the fold-out map accompanying this book (see below)

✉ address

☎ telephone number

🕐 opening times

🍽 restaurant or café on premises or near by

🚇 nearest Metro (underground) train station

🚃 nearest overground train station

♿ facilities for visitors with disabilities

💲 admission charge

↔ other nearby places of interest

❓ tours, lectures, or special events

➤ indicates the page where you will find a fuller description

MAPS
All map references are to the separate fold-out map accompanying this book. For example, the National Zoological Park at 3001 Connecticut Avenue NW has the following information: ✚ E1 – indicating the grid square of the map in which the National Zoological Park will be found. All entries within the Top 25 Sights section are also plotted by number (not page number) on the downtown plan located on the inside front and back covers of this book.

PRICES
Where appropriate, an indication of the cost of an establishment is given by $ signs: $$$ denotes higher prices, $$ denotes average prices, while $ denotes lower charges.

WASHINGTON *life*

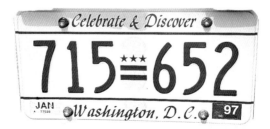

A PERSONAL VIEW

Washington is low and wide, with neo-classical federal buildings setting a tone for the memorial core which resonates throughout the city. Architecturally, the most demanding buildings take eclectic beaux-arts forms, stimulated by the 1893 Columbian Exposition and the McMillan Plan for Washington of 1901. Earlier buildings tend to be smaller, less showy and in late Georgian, Federal or Gothic Revival style. Post-World War II buildings incline toward standardised, undistinguished, monotonous presentations marching along the streets and avenues like the bureaucrats in short sleeves visible on any summer day in downtown Washington.

The Metro

The underground Metro system, opened in 1976 as a sort of bicentennial gift to the nation, is clean, generally safe and aesthetically pleasing. Washingtonians use the escalators as urban exercise machines and protocol requires that you stand right, walk left.

Washington's street grid uses the US Capitol as the orienting point: lettered (A–W) streets run east and west, numbered streets run north and south. Wide diagonal avenues, many ennobled and confused by memorial circles and squares,

The impressive Lincoln Memorial

are usually named after states. Two-and three-storey, brick and stone terraced houses, 14 to 18 feet wide, line neighbourhood streets. Originally single family dwellings, many of these Victorian houses now have an apartment, tucked into a basement or carved from unused space. More people make parking difficult; in Adams-Morgan, Dupont Circle, Georgetown and near the National Mall, parking is impossible.

Washington is peopled by transients who have lived here for decades. They come with the diplomatic corps and stay to see their grandchildren graduate from college. They are swept into the capital city on the coat-tails of an unexpected political win, and they live out their careers in the shadow of the Capitol dome. They move from New York to undertake political liaison for the banks, or they lobby for the Deep South industries of cotton, tobacco or sugar, and manage associations of lumbermen, airline pilots, toxicologists, women missionaries and uniformed workers. Since the rest of the country disdains Washington, they are often slightly embarrassed about staying, but they are attracted by the challenge, by the intellectual stimulation and by the raw power.

Washingtonians take the role of national host with good grace and they can be counted on for good directions and leisure-time ideas. This guide skims Washington's attractions and the reader should plan extra time to explore the sights, shops and streetscapes alluded to here.

Spring at the
National Arboretum

Segregation

Washington remains segregated, black from white. Georgetown and the upper northwest are white, Anacostia and northeast are black. Only Capitol Hill and Adams-Morgan have achieved a racial mix, and this is a fragile and uneasy condition. Seventy per cent of Washington's 600,000 residents are black.

7

WASHINGTON IN FIGURES

GENERAL
- Number of motor vehicles: 224,733
- Number of radio stations: 54
- Number of broadcast television stations: 8
- Number of cinemas: 58, at 17 locations
- Date became capital: 10 June 1800

BUILDINGS
- Maximum height of any building on Pennsylvania Avenue between the White House and the Capitol: 160 feet
- Oldest and largest Jesuit college in the US: Georgetown University, founded in 1789
- Largest Catholic church in the US: National Shrine of the Immaculate Conception
- Oldest surviving structure: the Old Stone House, 3051 M Street NW, begun 1764
- World's tallest masonry structure: Washington Monument, 555 feet
- World's tallest Corinthian columns: National Building Museum, 75 feet

GEOGRAPHY
- Latitude: 38 degrees, 52 minutes
- Longitude: 77 degrees, 00 minutes
- Elevation: 1 foot (near the Potomac River) to 410 feet (Tenley Town area of Upper Northwest)
- Area: 61 square miles
- Distance by air to:
  New York: 205 miles
  Los Angeles: 2,300 miles
  London: 3,674 miles
  Berlin: 4,181 miles
- Driving distance to:
  New York: 233 miles
  Los Angeles: 2,631 miles

PEOPLE
- The first year residents were allowed to vote in a Presidential election: 1964
- Population (1990): 606,900
- Population (1992): 585,221
- Per capita income: $25,363
- Number of colleges and universities: 6
- Largest employer: the federal government (about 240,000 civilian and military employees)
- Number of federal employees on Capitol Hill: 20,000

WASHINGTON PEOPLE

KATHARINE GRAHAM

Katharine Graham is one of Washington's élite. Currently chairman of the executive committee of The Washington Post Co., she has served at various times as chairman of the board, chief executive officer, president and publisher of Washington's leading daily newspaper.

Graham was born in New York in 1917. Educated at Vassar and the University of Chicago, she became a reporter for the *San Francisco News*. She later joined the *Washington Post* (a newspaper her father, Eugene Meyer, purchased at a bankruptcy sale in 1933) and worked in the editorial and circulation departments. Her husband, Philip L Graham, was publisher of the *Post* until his death in 1963. At that time, Mrs Graham suddenly found herself in charge of a major newspaper and unsure of her ability to run it. However, she chose staff wisely, chief among them Benjamin C Bradlee, whom she lured away from *Newsweek* and appointed executive editor. It was Bradlee, with Graham's support, who firmly established the *Post* in the 1970s as one of the country's leading newspapers with its breaking stories on the Watergate scandal and its publishing of the Pentagon Papers.

HAL GORDON

'I was wondering, asking the Lord really, what I was going to do with my time after retirement, when I stumbled over a snow mound and discovered a nearly frozen man. "Do this," came the answer.' And from that moment, Hal Gordon – retired army officer and bureaucrat, civil rights worker, Christian, husband, business developer, golfer – began learning how to touch the lives of homeless, addicted men and women. Today, the Community Action Group, with Gordon at its helm, houses, feeds, counsels, employs, encourages and celebrates the recovery and return to citizenship of about 100 people a year.

Larry Bowers

Larry Bowers explains city living on Capitol Hill like 'living in the eye of a storm'. After tiring of country dentistry, he bought a small neighbourhood practice in Washington, lived upstairs and dated Susan, the woman who would become his life partner. Eventually, they purchased a solid stone building on East Capitol Street which has been used as a physician's office since it was built in 1886. There was no backyard, so they built a roof deck which their two boys, Langly and Casey, clutter with rollerblades and hockey sticks, and which Susan uses for container gardening. You might see Larry playing rollerblade hockey with the kids on the playground across from Eastern Market on Saturday mornings.

A CHRONOLOGY

1790 President George Washington is authorised by Congress to build a Federal City

1791 Washington hires Pierre Charles L'Enfant to design a city on the banks of the Potomac River, siting, according to legend, the US Capitol in the exact centre of the 13 original states

1800 President Adams occupies the unfinished White House and Congress meets in the US Capitol, also unfinished. Population now 3,000

1812 US declares war on Britain

1814 The British sack Washington, burning many public buildings including the White House and the Capitol. Original Library of Congress burnt

1844 Samuel F B Morse transmits first telegraph from US Capitol to Baltimore, MD

1846 Congress accepts James Smithson's bequest and establishes Smithsonian Institution to 'increase and diffuse knowledge'

1850 Slave trade abolished in the District

1863 Lincoln issues the Emancipation Proclamation, freeing the nation's slaves. This begins an influx of former slaves to the nation's capital

1867 Howard University is chartered by Congress to teach African Americans

1876 The nation's centennial is celebrated with a fair in Philadelphia. Fifty-six train cars are filled with material to be donated to the Smithsonian. The District's population is about 140,000

1901 President McKinley authorises the McMillan Commission to oversee the beautification of the city

1908 Trains diverted to the new Union Station, which includes a Presidential Waiting Room for diplomatic and security purposes

1917 US enters World War I; the population reaches 400,000 as the city enjoys a wartime boom

1939 Marian Anderson gives free concert at the Lincoln Memorial, after being denied the stage at DAR Constitution Hall because of her race

1941 US enters World War II; the city enters a boom

1958 East Front extension of the US Capitol begins, adding 102 offices

1961 President John F Kennedy plans renovation and rejuvenation of Pennsylvania Avenue. Residents are given right to vote in presidential elections

1963 Martin Luther King, Jr delivers his 'I have a dream' speech from the Lincoln Memorial

1968 King delivers his last sermon at Washington National Cathedral. His shooting in Memphis five days later sparks riots and areas of the city are burned, particularly along the U Street corridor

1968–73 Anti-war demonstrations on the National Mall

1974 Watergate Hotel becomes infamous as the site of the bungled Republican robbery attempt on Democratic headquarters. President Richard Nixon resigns as a result of the ensuing cover-up

1976 Many of the Bicentennial celebrations are focused on Washington. Metrorail opens and becomes an immediate transport success

1981 President Ronald Reagan is shot outside his car at the Washington Hilton

1984 The renovated Old Post Office reopens and revives this section of Pennsylvania Avenue

1988 The renovated Union Station reopens

1990 Washington National Cathedral is completed after 73 years. Mayor Sharon Pratt Dixon Kelly is the first black woman to head a major US city

1993 US Holocaust Memorial Museum opens

1995 White House Information Center opens

11

PEOPLE & EVENTS FROM HISTORY

'Duke' Ellington

Edward Kennedy Ellington, born in 1899, grew up in Washington (► 50). Generally recognised as the most influential American composer, Ellington concerned himself with jazz composition and musical form, as distinct from improvisation, writing and arranging. He also sustained and supported an orchestra to perform his incomparable music. Upon his death in 1974, the Duke Ellington School for the Arts was established in his honour.

FREDERICK LAW OLMSTED SR

Born in 1822, the nation's first and foremost landscape architect began work on the grounds of the US Capitol in 1874. He is credited with creating the vast sweep of lawn and trees of the west front. The Olmsted Walk at the National Zoological Park leads past the animals and gives a good sense of Olmsted's genius for naturalistic environments. In 1866 Olmsted designed the grounds of Gallaudet University, the country's first university for the hearing-impaired. At Olmsted's tireless insistence, Congress passed legislation to safeguard Rock Creek as the park that we enjoy today. Olmsted died in 1903.

MARY McLEOD BETHUNE

Daughter of slaves, presidential advisor, energetic teacher, advocate for young people and champion of human rights, Mary McLeod Bethune (1875–1955) founded the Daytona Normal and Industrial Institute for Negro Girls (now Bethune-Cookman College) and the National Council of Negro Women. Her impact on Washington was commemorated in 1974 with the dedication of the Bethune Memorial in Lincoln Park. As a tribute to Bethune's work for black women and children, Thomas Ball's bronze sculpture, *Emancipation*, in Lincoln Park since 1876, was resited to face Robert Berk's bronze of Ms. Bethune. Her home houses the Bethune Museum and Archives (► 54).

A DREAM OF EQUALITY

On 28 August 1963 Martin Luther King Jr delivered his vision of racial harmony and equality from the steps of the Lincoln Memorial to a crowd of 200,000. King, born in 1929, set up the first black ministry in Alabama in 1955 and became the figurehead of a non-violent civil rights movement fighting to end segregation and discrimination. His "I have a dream..." speech was the culmination of a march on Washington D.C. by blacks and whites calling for reform. King won the Nobel Peace Prize in 1964. He was assassinated four years later.

WASHINGTON
how to organise your time

13

ITINERARIES

Tourist sites and shops do not open much before 10AM. Use the Metro: parking is difficult and expensive (downtown meters are now 25 cents for 7½ minutes!). The Metro is fast, efficient, generally safe and inexpensive, but remember that it closes at midnight. Do not be afraid of taxi travel; it, too, is safe and cheap. Taxis can be flagged easily in tourist areas.

ITINERARY ONE

CAPITOL HILL & GEORGETOWN

First light

Join the crowd of joggers who pound the pavements and paths in the memorial core.

Morning

Visit the US Capitol (➤ 43), Supreme Court (➤ 45) and Library of Congress (➤ 46).

Lunch

Enjoy the view and lunch in Library of Congress's Madison Building cafeteria.

Afternoon

Walk down the hill to the Botanic Gardens (➤ 42) or the National Air and Space Museum (➤ 41).

Evening

Take a cab to Washington Harbour, 3000 K Street NW, Georgetown (➤ 18), the post-modern extravaganza with boardwalk, restaurants, offices and flats.

ITINERARY TWO

ART, ARCHIVES, AIR & SPACE

Morning

Visit the National Archives (➤ 39) and National Gallery of Art (➤ 40).

Lunch

National Gallery of Art.

Afternoon

Visit the National Air and Space Museum (➤ 41) or National Museum of Natural History or, for more art, try the four Smithsonian museums clustered near the Castle, 900 Jefferson Drive (➤ 36): Hirshhorn Museum and Sculpture Garden, National Museum of African Art, Sackler and Freer Galleries.

Evening

Have a pre-theatre dinner and see a show at the Kennedy Center (➤ 25).

ITINERARY THREE	**AROUND THE TIDAL BASIN**
Morning	Visit the US Holocaust Memorial Museum (➤ 33).
Lunch	Kosher Cafeteria at the Holocaust Memorial Museum.
Afternoon	Visit the Bureau of Engraving and Printing (➤ 35); stroll around the Tidal Basin and visit the Jefferson Memorial (➤ 32), and then the Lincoln Memorial (➤ 26).
Evening	Take a cab to Union Station (➤ 44) for dinner, shopping, or a movie.
ITINERARY FOUR	**WHITE HOUSE & DUPONT CIRCLE**
Morning	Start at the White House Information Center (➤ 30) and after a tour of 1600 Pennsylvania Avenue, visit the FBI Building (➤ 37).
Lunch	Take Metro to Dupont Circle and lunch at Dupont Circle Underground fast-food court.
Afternoon	Explore the small museums, embassies and shops in and around Dupont Circle (➤ 17). Dupont Circle seems to have more coffee shops per capita than anywhere else in Washington: people-watch in a sidewalk café then browse in the bookstores – some open all night.
Evening	Have dinner in Adams-Morgan (➤ 18) and dance the night away.

Dupont Circle café

WALKS

INFORMATION

Time 2¾ hours
Distance 1½ miles
Start point US Capitol
⊞ J5
Ⓜ Capitol South
End point White House
⊞ F4
Ⓜ McPherson Square

Freedom Plaza

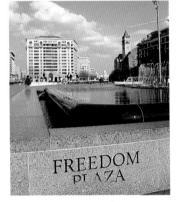

FREEDOM PLAZA

PATH OF PRESIDENTS: A WALK FROM THE CAPITOL TO THE WHITE HOUSE

Immediately following the Inauguration, the President and his entourage descend the west face of the Capitol and proceed in bullet-proof cars up Pennsylvania Avenue to the White House. This tour takes the same route.

Begin on the west steps of the Capitol building, overlooking the wide, grassy swath of the National Mall. The view takes in the memorial core of Washington, from the Botanic Gardens and federal office buildings on the left along Maryland Avenue, to the Washington Monument and Lincoln Memorial directly ahead, to the domes of the National Museum of Natural History and National Gallery of Art, and the Federal Triangle complex on the right.

Follow Pennsylvania Avenue, passing or exploring the National Gallery of Art, the Canadian Embassy, the National Archives and the Navy Memorial. Turn right onto the thriving art corridor of 7th Street, left in front of the National Portrait Gallery and left on 10th Street past Ford's Theatre, where Abraham Lincoln was fatally wounded on 14 April 1865. The bully building of the FBI is on the left.

Turn right on to Pennsylvania Avenue. The clock tower of the Old Post Office offers an unsurpassed city view. Further up Pennsylvania is Freedom Plaza, with its incised stone map of L'Enfant's city plan, and Pershing Park serving as a front yard to the Willard Hotel and to the White House Information Center. Turn right on 15th Street, past the 1836 Treasury Building, which you will recognise because it appears on the $10 bill, and left onto Pennsylvania Avenue in front of the White House.

WALKS

DUPONT CIRCLE: DISCOVER COSMOPOLITAN WASHINGTON

Dupont Circle is the heart of single, chic Washington, and a focus for gay culture. Clubs, restaurants, book stores, urbane coffee shops and boutiques line Connecticut Avenue and P Street on both sides of the Circle, though the Circle itself is home to the homeless. Distinctive small museums and art galleries, embassies and important architecture are included on this tour.

Begin at the Q Street exit to the Dupont Circle Metro. Go east on Q to 1700 where Thomas Franklin Schneider's robust terraced houses animate the street. The 1894-built steel-framed Cairo at 1615 Q prompted Congress to introduce height restrictions. Turn south on 17th Street and right onto the residential Church Street. Turn left on 18th Street and right on P to the ornate Patterson House. The architecturally successful Euram Building at 21 Dupont Circle encloses a magnificent courtyard.

Turn left onto New Hampshire Avenue to 1307, the Historical Society of Washington. Take a right on to 20th Street then turn left on to Massachusetts Avenue. On the left is The Walsh Mansion, purchased by Indonesia in 1951 for one-tenth of its original 1903 cost of $3,000,000. At 1600 21st Street is the Phillips Collection. Continue to 2118 Massachusetts Avenue past the walled courtyard of the 1902–1905 Anderson House. In the 2200 block and Sheridan Circle, you will encounter many embassies.

Turn right on S Street, stopping if time allows at Woodrow Wilson House and the Textile Museum. Walk down the delightful Decatur Terrace Steps. Turn left onto Decatur Place, and left on Florida Avenue, then continue to Connecticut Avenue and on to Dupont Circle Metro.

Italian eating, Dupont Circle

THE SIGHTS

- Schneider's terraced houses
- The Cairo Apartment Building
- Patterson House
- Euram Building
- Historical Society of Washington (► 54)
- Walsh Mansion
- Indonesian Embassy
- Phillips Collection (► 27)
- Anderson House
- Cosmos Club
- Sheridan Circle
- Embassies of Togo, Sudan, Greece, Egypt, Kenya, Philippines
- Woodrow Wilson House
- Textile Museum
- Decatur Terrace Steps

INFORMATION

Time 1½ hours
Distance 2½ miles
Start and end point Dupont Circle
✚ F3
◉ Dupont Circle

17

EVENING STROLLS

ADAMS-MORGAN

Adams-Morgan takes its name from the all-white Adams and the all-black Morgan elementary schools. It occupies high ground in Washington, and adds each new wave of immigrants to its diverse mix. From the corner of 18th Street NW and Columbia Road walk two or three blocks in any direction day or night to encounter sidewalk cafés, shops, galleries and clubs. You can eat Mexican, Indian, Salvadorian, Ethiopian, French, Caribbean and Argentinian: just a few of the cuisines offered. You can dance at the Kilimanjaro (1724 California Street NW) or at one of the several restaurants which turn into lively dance clubs after 11PM.

GEORGETOWN

Take a cab to Washington Harbor, 3000 K Street NW, and explore this exuberant post-modern large-scale complex. You can have a meal here or just enjoy the fountains, outdoor sculpture and river-front boardwalk. Walk up 30th Street NW, stopping at the Chesapeake and Ohio Canal. During the day you can walk, jog, or bike for miles along the towpath. Walk a block further up the hill to M Street, a main commercial axis with small restaurants and boutiques. Go left two blocks to Wisconsin Avenue and the heart of Georgetown. Shopping for all tastes is here.

Georgetown

ORGANISED SIGHTSEEING

GRAY LINE TOURS

Gray Line Tours cover major Washington tourist sites including Embassy Row. Regular out-of-town excursions include Mount Vernon and Alexandria.

✉ 5500 Tuxedo Road, Tuxedo, MD 20781
☎ 301/386 8300, 800/353 6114, extension 320 ⊞ Prices vary with tour

Old Town Trolley Tour

NATIONAL BUILDING MUSEUM

The National Building Museum produces walking and bus tours about Washington architecture and construction.

✉ 401 F Street NW ☎ 202/272 2448 Ⓜ Judiciary Square ⊞ Prices vary with tour

NATIONAL PARK SERVICE

The National Park Service produces a brochure which describes the Black History National Recreation Trail.

✉ 1100 Ohio Drive SW, Washington DC 20242 ☎ 202/619 7222 ⊞ Free

OLD TOWN TROLLEY TOURS

Old Town Trolley Tours takes in the memorial core and also goes to Georgetown, the National Zoo and Washington Cathedral. Abbreviated evening tours available.

☎ 301/985 3021, 800/868 7482 ⊞ Moderate, children under five ride free

SMITHSONIAN ASSOCIATES

The Smithsonian Associates Program offers walking and bus tours through area neighbourhoods; often topical subjects – African-American life, beaux-arts architecture, public gardens, artists' studios – are addressed.

☎ 202/357 3030 ⊞ Prices vary with tour

TOURMOBILE

Tourmobile buses stop near most of the sites in this guide, including the Frederick Douglass National Historic Site.

☎ 202/554 7950, 202/554 5100 ♿ Wheel-chair-equipped vans available ⊞ Moderate, children under three ride free

Personal guides

For personal guides for individuals or groups, in almost any language, contact:

A Tour de Force
✉ Box 2782, Washington DC 20013
☎ 703/525 2948

DC Foot Tour
✉ Box 9001, Alexandria, VA 22304
☎ 703/461 7364

Guide Post, Inc.
✉ 9711 Saxony Road, Silver Spring, MD 20910
☎ 301/754 2402 Fax 202/754 2405

Guide Service of Washington
✉ 733 15th Street Suite 1040, Washington DC 20005
☎ 202/628 2842

Photographic guide

If photography is your thing, contact Sunny Odem, who guarantees the best holiday photographs you've ever taken:
✉ 2530D Walter Reed Drive, Arlington, VA
☎ 703/379 1633

EXCURSIONS

Old Town Alexandria

Ramsay House Visitors
Center offers extensive
information:

- ✉ 221 King Street
- ☎ 703/838 4200
- 🕐 Daily 9–5
- 🚇 King Street Station, then
  board Dash bus AT2 or AT5
  eastbound.
  By car 14th Street Bridge
  (toward National Airport),
  continue on George
  Washington Parkway to King
  Street
  By bike Start at the Lincoln
  Memorial and cross Memorial
  Bridge heading south 5.6
  miles to Alexandria.

Mount Vernon

- ☎ 703/780 2000
- 🕐 Daily 9–5
- 🍴 Mt Vernon Inn & Snack Bar
- 🚇 Pentagon, then bus 11P,
  11H, 11Y
- 🚌 Tourmobile and Gray Line
  Tours make daily trips
  By car 14th Street Bridge
  (to National Airport), then
  south on George Washington
  Memorial Parkway
  By bike Start at the Lincoln
  Memorial and cross Memorial
  Bridge heading south 17
  miles to Mount Vernon
- 🚢 *Potomac Spirit* from Pier 4,
  5th and Water Streets SE
- ☎ 202/554 8000
- 💲 Expensive
- 🕐 Oct–May, Tue–Sun 9:30;
  Jun–Sep, Tue–Sun 9:30, 2

OLD TOWN ALEXANDRIA, VA

Six miles south of Washington, Old Town Alexandria provides a good view of sophisticated, small-town America which has retained or restored its colonial seaport architecture and traditions. Start at the Ramsay House Visitors Center which will provide joint tickets, parking permits, walking guides, and restaurant and shopping recommendations. Old Town, which is easily walked, includes hundreds of colonial buildings, many of them open to the public. The Torpedo Factory Arts Center houses dozens of artisans, often available to discuss their work, and Historic Alexandria, which conducts archaeological research in the area.

MOUNT VERNON, VA

George Washington's ancestral estate, Mount Vernon, 17 miles south of Washington DC, is the most-visited historic house in the country. The Mount Vernon Ladies Association, formed in 1853 to preserve the estate, can also be credited with starting the historic preservation movement in the US. The mansion overlooks the Potomac River and is built of yellow pine painted to resemble stone. The ornate interior is furnished with decorative arts and memorabilia authentic to the last years of Washington's life. The outbuildings re-create spaces needed for an 18th-century self-sufficient farm, including smoke and laundry houses, external kitchen and slave quarters.

Old Town Alexandria

FREDERICKSBURG, VA

This historic town, 50 miles south of Washington on I-95, makes every effort to welcome visitors to its 40-block National Historic District containing the house George Washington bought his mother, James Monroe's law offices, a 1752 plantation, an early apothecary shop, and the Georgian architecture of Chatham Manor overlooking the Rappahannock River. Many Civil War battles were waged in and around Fredericksburg and you can hike the battlefields and nearby wilderness parks. The shopping streets offer antiques and rare-book shops and art galleries which support the historic character of this charming town. Start at the well-marked Visitors Center, which will provide maps and expert advice.

SOLOMONS, MD

This area retains much of its rural character and for that reason rewards an excursion, though a car is needed. Aim for the Information Center, 60 miles south of Washington, near the Calvert Marine Museum which offers quality exhibitions about the Chesapeake Bay, commercial fishing, maritime history and estuarine biology. The town offers a pleasant three-block river walk where you are likely to encounter several varieties of ducks, historic churches, quaint B & Bs, modern hotels, fishing, seafood restaurants and a well-maintained wetlands nature park and beach.

George Washington's estate, Mount Vernon

INFORMATION

Fredericksburg Visitors Center
- ✉ 706 Caroline Street, Fredericksburg
- ☎ 703/373 1776, 800/678 4748
- 🕐 Daily 9–5
- 🚆 Amtrak from Union Station. About 1¼ hours travel time.
  By car south on I-95 to Exit 130A and follow the signs to the Visitors Center
- ☎ 202/484 7540, 800/872 7245

Solomons Information Center
- ✉ Rt 2, Solomons
- ☎ 410/326 6027
- 🕐 Daily 9–5
  By car Pennsylvania Avenue South, which turns into Rt 4.
  Follow the signs for Calvert Marine Museum and Solomons Island

21

What's On

JANUARY	*Washington Antiques Show* (☎ 202/234 0700)
FEBRUARY	*African American History Month* (☎ 202/789 2403) *Lincoln's Birthday* (☎ 202/619 7222) *Chinese New Year* (☎ 202/724 4091)
MARCH	*St Patrick's Day Festival* (☎ 202/347 1450) *Organist's Bach Marathon* (☎ 202/363 2202)
APRIL	*National Cherry Blossom Festival* (☎ 202/728 1137) *White House Spring Garden Tour* (☎ 202/456 7041)
MAY	*Washington National Cathedral Flower Mart* (☎ 202/537 6200) *Georgetown Garden Tour* (☎ 202/333 6896)
JUNE	*Shakespeare Free For All* (☎ 202/628 5770) *Big Band Concert Series* (☎ 202/619 7222)
JULY	*Smithsonian Festival of American Folklife* (☎ 202/357 2700) *Hispanic Festival* (☎ 202/822 9293)
AUGUST	Everybody's at the beach
SEPTEMBER	*National Symphony Orchestra Labor Day Concert* (☎ 202/467 4600) *Adams-Morgan Day* (☎ 202/332 3292)
OCTOBER	*Washington International Horse Show* (☎ 301/840 0281) *Marine Corps Marathon* (☎ 703/690 3431)
NOVEMBER	*Veterans Day Activities* (☎ 202/475 0843) *Thanksgiving Day Holiday*
DECEMBER	*Annual Scottish Christmas Walk* (☎ 703/838 4200) *US Botanic Gardens Poinsettia Show* (☎ 202/225 7099) *People's Christmas Tree Lighting* (☎ 202/224 6645)

WASHINGTON's
top 25 sights

The sights are numbered from west to east across the city

ARLINGTON NATIONAL CEMETERY

HIGHLIGHTS

- Kennedy graves
- Memorial Amphitheater
- Tomb of the Unknowns
- Custis-Lee Mansion
- L'Enfant's grave
- Medgar Evers' grave
- USS Marine Memorial
- Shuttle *Challenger*
- Astronauts Memorial
- Changing of the Guard at the Tomb of the Unknowns
- 49-bell Netherlands Carillon

INFORMATION

- ✚ C6/D6/C7/D7
- ✉ ANC, Arlington, VA 22211
- ☎ 703/692 0931
- ◉ Apr–Sep, daily 8–7; Oct–Mar, daily 8–5
- ▣ Arlington Cemetery
- ▣ Tourmobile
- ♿ Excellent. Disabled visitors may board Tourmobile Shuttles or obtain driving permit at the Visitors Center
- ▨ Free
- ❓ Narrated Tourmobile Shuttle, every 20 mins. Car parking ($) available at the cemetery

" *The most visited gravesite in the US, that of John F Kennedy, can be found on a hillside overlooking the capital city in the 612 acres of Arlington National Cemetery. President Kennedy's grave makes this a mecca for Americans who came of age in the 1960s, but Arlington shelters veterans from every American conflict.* **"**

History The first burial at the Tomb of the Unknowns occurred on 11 November 1921. This World War I soldier was joined in 1958 by honoured dead from World War II and Korea and, in 1984, by a Vietnam veteran.

Under an eternal flame, John F Kennedy lies next to his wife Jacqueline Bouvier Kennedy Onassis and two of his children who died in infancy. Near by lies his brother, Robert Kennedy, slain in a similar act of senseless violence in 1968. Robert Kennedy's grave is marked by a simple white cross and a fountain, which overflows itself in the form of a quiet water curtain.

What to see Above the Kennedy graves stands the Greek-Revival Custis-Lee Mansion (also known as Arlington House), built between 1802 and 1817 by George Washington Parke Custis, grandson of Martha and step-grandson of George Washington. Just off the west corner of the house lies the grave of Pierre L'Enfant, now overlooking for eternity the Federal City which he designed with political difficulty and dispute enough to leave him a penniless and embittered man. Throughout the cemetery simple markers march along like the soldiers themselves, many of whom are now joined by their wives.

KENNEDY CENTER

❝Strolling the roof terrace of the Kennedy Center provides a magnificent 360–degree view of Washington and the Potomac River, and may turn a potentially boring intermission into a romantic interlude.❞

History Opened in 1971, Edward Durrell Stone's simple white marble box overlooks the Potomac River and is situated next to the eccentric Watergate complex, infamous as the site of the bungled attempt to bug the Democratic National Committee which eventually led to the resignation of President Richard Nixon.

When the Kennedy Center opened, the space for performance arts in Washington stepped up to world-class quality. The opera house and concert hall, in particular, have splendid acoustics.

What to see The building accommodates an opera house, two stage theatres, a theatre lab, a concert hall, a film theatre, and the Performance Art Library of the Library of Congress. Many of these can be seen on a tour of the building, or at intermission during a performance.

The building is sheathed in 3,700 tons of white Carrara marble, a gift from Italy. The Grand Foyer, 630 feet long and 60 feet high, blazes with the light of 18 Orrefors crystal chandeliers, donated by Sweden and reflected in 60-foot-high mirrors, a gift from Belgium. Overlooking the theatre-goers is a bust of President Kennedy by Robert Berks, artist also for the whimsical Albert Einstein Memorial. Elsewhere, the Hall of States displays state flags arranged in the order the states joined the Union.

HIGHLIGHTS

- Hall of States
- View from the roof terrace
- Bust of John F Kennedy
- Painted biblical scenes in the Israeli Lounge
- Henri Matisse tapestries, a gift from France

INFORMATION

- ✚ E 4/5
- ✉ New Hampshire Avenue at Rock Creek Parkway NW
- ☎ 202/467 4600; 800/444 1324
- ◉ Daily for tours and performances as scheduled
- 🍽 Encore Café 11–8; Roof Terrace Restaurant 5:30–9
- Ⓢ Foggy Bottom
- ♿ Excellent
- 🎟 Free tours; performance ticket prices vary
- ⟷ Watergate Hotel (► 84), Georgetown (► 18)
- ❓ One hour tours between 10AM and 1PM

Matisse tapestry

3

THE LINCOLN MEMORIAL

HIGHLIGHTS

- Daniel Chester French's *Lincoln*
- Inscription of Lincoln's 1863 Gettysburg Address and Second Inaugural speech
- Underground exhibit on First Amendment rights
- Reflecting Pool
- View

INFORMATION

- ✚ E5
- ✉ The Mall at 23rd Street NW
- ☎ 202/426 6841
- 🕐 Open 24 hours, staffed 8AM–midnight
- Ⓜ Foggy Bottom
- ♿ Excellent
- ▣ Free
- ↔ Jefferson Memorial (➤ 32), Vietnam Veterans Memorial (➤ 28)
- ❓ Tours available upon request

❝*Fittingly, a century after Lincoln emancipated the slaves, Martin Luther King Jr delivered his famous 'I have a dream' speech on the steps of the Lincoln Memorial.***❞**

History John Wilkes Booth shot Abraham Lincoln in Ford's Theatre on 14 April 1865. Lincoln died the next day. Four decades passed before congressional and public support reached a consensus on the design and siting of a monument befitting the nation's most important abolitionist. Work began on the Lincoln Memorial on the eve of World War I and continued until 1922, when Henry Bacon's Greek temple was dedicated.

What to see The 36 columns symbolise the 36 states in the Union when Lincoln died. The names of the 48 states in the Union in 1922, at the time of the monument's dedication, are inscribed above the parapet's crowning frieze. Daniel Chester French's 8-ton, 19-foot marble statue captures a contemplative Lincoln; so powerful and sombre is the statue that one can easily imagine Lincoln rising up and resuming his epic struggles in a Washington still sadly segregated even today. A small museum on the lower level chronicles the monument's construction. The view from the monument steps at sunset is one of the most romantic in the city, as the Washington Monument stands reflected in the rectangular pool created for this purpose.

The colonnaded façade of the Lincoln Memorial

4

PHILLIPS COLLECTION

"Washington has distinguished museums beyond the memorial core, including the first permanent modern art museum in America, known as the Phillips Collection. Listening to chamber music in these intimate galleries on Sunday evenings provides the perfect end to a get-away weekend."

History In 1921 Duncan Phillips opened two gallery rooms in his intimate Georgian-Revival mansion as a memorial to his father and brother. An enlarged and renovated annexe retaining a domestic scale was opened in 1989, and provides additional space for travelling exhibitions and for items from the permanent collection, changing periodically.

Duncan Phillips married a painter, Marjorie Acker, and together they carefully assembled an unparalleled collection of French Impressionists, Post-Impressionists, Cubists, 17th- and 18th-century masters, and American Modernists. They sought out those paintings which glowed with an artist's unique vision; their avoidance of the merely average lends a special quality to the collection.

What to see The playful Swiss painter, Paul Klee, is well represented here, as is the master of brilliant domestic images, Pierre Bonnard. Americans Arthur Dove, Georgia O'Keeffe, and Mark Rothko co-exist peacefully alongside Picasso, Monet, and Degas. The paintings are hung in simple domestic settings, and throughout the building art students serve as security specialists and are always willing and able to discuss the works of art in detail. From autumn until spring on Sunday afternoons concerts are held in the music room.

HIGHLIGHTS

- *Luncheon of the Boating Party*, Renoir
- Works by Paul Klee
- *Repentant Peter*, El Greco
- *Entrance to the Public Garden at Arles*, Van Gogh
- *Dancers at the Bar*, Degas
- American Modernists
- Pierre Bonnard collection

INFORMATION

- ✚ E3
- ✉ 1600–1612 21st Street NW
- ☎ 202/387 2151
- ⏱ Mon–Sat 10–5; Sun 12–7; also Thu 5–8
- 🍴 Café
- Ⓜ Dupont Circle
- ♿ Excellent
- 🎫 Moderate Sat, Sun; contributions Mon–Fri
- ❓ Tours Wed and Sat 2PM

Top: Luncheon of the Boating Party *by Pierre Auguste Renoir (1881)*

27

5

VIETNAM VETERANS MEMORIAL

HIGHLIGHTS

- Inscribed names
- Frederick Hart's sculptural group
- Glenna Goodacre's sculptural group
- The city reflected in the polished stone

INFORMATION

- E5
- Near Constitution Avenue between 21st and 22nd Streets, NW
- 202/634 1568
- Open 24 hours, staffed 8AM—midnight
- Foggy Bottom
- Excellent
- Free
- Presidents' Monuments (➤ 26, 31, 32); Albert Einstein Memorial (➤ 57)
- Rangers available to assist in locating names and provide paper and graphite suitable for taking an imprint of the names

Names on the Wall

"*The Vietnam Veterans Memorial has been called the most moving memorial in Washington, and on most days there is an almost constant procession of quiet visitors moving down into the 'black gash of shame', as one veteran characterised it.*"

History Maya Ying Lin's design is simplicity itself: two triangular stone walls set at a 125-degree angle, and sited between the Washington Monument and Lincoln Memorial. At its apex the walls taper to 10 feet in height and seem to overpower the visitors standing beneath them. The names of heroes who made the ultimate sacrifice for their country are placed chronologically: more than 58,000 killed or missing in action from 1956 to 1975, the longest war in American history.

What to see The polished black granite reflects sky, trees, nearby monuments and the faces of visitors as they search for the names of fathers, sons and loved ones. Each day National Park Service Rangers collect the mementoes left near a soldier's name: letters, uniforms, military emblems and photographs. These tokens receive the care of museum acquisitions and are held by the National Park Service in perpetuity as part of the history of the nation.

The Wall, as it is commonly called, was thought by some veterans insufficient to represent them. In 1984 Frederick Hart's slightly larger-than-life sculpture of three soldiers was dedicated, sited at one of the entrances to the Wall. The Vietnam Veterans Women's Memorial – a figural sculpture by Glenna Goodacre – was dedicated near by on Veterans Day, 1993.

NATIONAL GEOGRAPHIC SOCIETY

"Walk into any international company's Washington office and you are likely to see a 6-foot-high map of the world pinned with the locations of the missions, projects and plants of the enterprise. These maps, an affectation of the frequent-flyer set, invariably come from the National Geographic Society.**"**

History Since 1888 the Society has increased and diffused geographic knowledge as directed by its charter. Even today, the familiar yellow monthly *National Geographic* may be the only current information about life beyond the US borders that many American school-children receive.

What to see Explorers Hall is located on the first floor of Edward Durrell's glass and marble 10-storey building. Architectural buffs notice the similarities to the Kennedy Center, also designed by Durrell. *Geographica*, a high-tech, celebratory exhibit installed for National Geo's centennial in 1988, allows you to touch a tornado, explore a Martian landscape, test your knowledge of early human development, investigate undersea archaeology and gawp at space trivia. The world's largest free-standing globe, 11 feet tall and 34 feet in circumference, shows Earth at a scale of 1 inch to 60 miles. There are short films, one narrated by Leonard Nimoy of *Star Trek* fame, and an interactive amphitheatre which simulates orbital flight and looks at Earth from space. Exhibits are enhanced by exquisite, large-format images taken by the Society's award-winning photographers. In the gift shop, you can buy the Society's many publications: maps, books, videos and CD-ROMs.

HIGHLIGHTS

- World's largest free-standing globe
- Touch a tornado
- Earth Station One
- Holographic images
- Rock and water courtyard
- Model of Jacques Cousteau's diving saucer
- Admiral Robert E Perry's dog sledge
- Moon rock
- National Geo TV Room

INFORMATION

- ✚ F3
- ✉ 17th and M Streets NW
- ☎ 202/857 7588
- ⏰ Mon–Sat 9–5, Sun 10–5
- Ⓜ Dupont Circle, Farragut North
- ♿ Excellent
- 🎫 Free

7

WHITE HOUSE

INFORMATION

- ✚ F4
- ✉ 1600 Pennsylvania Avenue
- ☎ 202/456 7041
- 🕐 Tue–Sat 10AM–noon
- 🚇 McPherson Square, Metro
  Center
- ♿ Excellent
- 🎫 Free
- ❓ For free timed tickets and
  historical exhibitions, call
  in at the White House
  Information Center in
  the Department of
  Commerce Building,
  15th and H Streets NW
  Arrive at the White House
  Information Center by 8AM
  for a chance of tickets that
  day

"Virtually every desk, tea service, silver platter, decanter, painting and floor covering in the house intertwines with the historic events, writ large and small, of the American democracy."

History Despite the fact that Thomas Jefferson called James Hogan's original design 'big enough for two emperors, one Pope, and the grand Lama', when he became the second occupant of 1600 Pennsylvania Avenue in 1801, Jefferson designed and added colonnaded wings to house domestic and office functions. Today the White House looks modest, flanked as it is by the US Treasury, the largest Greek-Revival building anywhere in the world, and the 10-acre Old Executive Office Building, memorably described by President Harry Truman as 'the greatest monstrosity in America'. The British burned the White House in 1814 and the rebuilding which followed was only one of several renovations conducted over the years by First Families.

What to see Each occupant has left his mark until, today, the President's house holds an impressive display of decorative arts from the Sheraton, French (and American) Empire periods, Queen Anne and Federal periods. There are carved Carrara marble mantels, Bohemian cut-glass chandeliers, Turkish Hereke carpets, and elaborate plasterwork throughout, as well as 18 acres of gardens. The exact programme of a White House tour may vary because of the conduct of official business. Usually open to visitors are the ceremonial East Room, a small drawing-room known as the Green Room, the Blue and Red Rooms (known for their superb French Empire furnishings) and the neo-classical State Dining Room.

THE WASHINGTON MONUMENT

"Children, in particular, enjoy the 70-second lift-ride to the pinnacle of this, the highest structure in Washington, where a wide perspective on the District, Maryland and Virginia can be gained."

History The Washington Monument punctuates the axis of the White House and Jefferson Memorial and the US Congress and Lincoln Memorial, a perfect example of how government projects can go awry. A 1783 Congressional resolution called for an equestrian statue to honour George Washington for his heroic leadership during the American Revolution. Nothing happened until 1836, when private citizens formed the Washington National Monument Society and solicited one dollar from every living American. Having raised $28,000, the group laid the cornerstone to Robert Mills' design in 1848. The Civil War interrupted work on the obelisk; construction did not resume again until the national fervour surrounding the Centennial of the American Revolution in 1876. The interruption is evident in the change in the marble's colour 150 feet from the ground.

What to see Five-hundred-and-fifty-five feet, five-and-a-half inches of marble obelisk comprise the monument. The view from the top encompasses most of the District and parts of Maryland and Virginia: spy out the Tidal Basin, the Jefferson and Lincoln memorials, the White House, the US Capitol, the Library of Congress and the Smithsonian Institution. Visitors who take the guided walk down the monument's 898 steps, instead of going down in the lift, can see the commemorative plaques donated during construction by states, masonic lodges, church groups and foreign countries. The queues tend to be shorter at night.

HIGHLIGHTS

- Views from the top
- Plaques

INFORMATION

- ✚ F5/G5
- ✉ The Mall at 15th Street NW
- ☎ 202/426 6840
- 🕐 Apr–Labor Day, daily 8AM–midnight; Labor Day–Mar, daily 9–5
- 🍴 Smithsonian
- ♿ Excellent
- 🎫 Free
- 🚇 Smithsonian Institution (► 36), Memorials (► 26, 28, 32)
- ❓ 'Down the Steps' guided tours Sat and Sun 10 and 2

The 555ft obelisk

9

THE JEFFERSON MEMORIAL

HIGHLIGHTS

- Jefferson bronze
- Inscribed Declaration of Independence
- Jefferson's statement on the separation of Church and State
- Japanese lantern on Kurtz Bridge
- Exhibit on Jefferson's inventions
- Cherry blossoms in April

INFORMATION

- F6
- South bank of the Tidal Basin
- 202/426 6821
- Daily 8AM–midnight
- Smithsonian Metro (20-minute walk)
- Excellent
- Free

The Tidal Basin

"MNMT VW. Freshmen members of Congress decipher these initials in the classified section of The Washington Post when choosing a place to live: Monument View. Washington orients by the memorials."

History The Jefferson Memorial forms a north-south axis with the White House and like virtually all building projects in Washington, it caused controversy in the capital city. John Russell Pope's design adapted Rome's Pantheon in deference to Jefferson's love of classical architecture. Jefferson, an amateur architect himself, had used similar circular domed structures at his home, Monticello, and at the University of Virginia. But Pope's design was derided as antique by important Washingtonians. Others argued that Jefferson's philosophy dictated a more utilitarian structure, perhaps an amphitheatre. Eventually, Pope's design was dedicated in 1943 on Jefferson's 200th birthday.

What to see A wide plaza overlooks the Tidal Basin, and formal stairs lead up through a pedimented portico, surrounded by an Ionic colonnade encircling the open centre. The pediment supports sculpted marble figures of Jefferson, Benjamin Franklin, John Adams, Roger Sherman and Robert Livingston, members of the Constitution-drafting committee. Rudolph Evans produced the 19-foot bronze sculpture of Jefferson standing in the centre, which is surrounded by excerpts of his speeches and writings carved into the walls. In April, blossoming cherry trees frame the memorial.

US HOLOCAUST MEMORIAL MUSEUM

"This museum sets new standards for museum design, historical interpretation, purpose-built architecture and visitor services. To almost everyone's surprise, however, the museum continues to be over-subscribed and visitors require timed tickets."

History 'You cannot deal with the Holocaust as a reasonable thing' explained architect James Ingo Freed. To that end, he created a discordant building, dedicated in 1993, intended to disturb the classical façades and placid faces seen everywhere in Washington.

What to see Watch towers line the north and south walls and contribute to the prison-like atmosphere of the building. This prevails throughout, in the exposed beams, metal railings and malevolent elevators. Everywhere one looks or stands there is a memory or a nightmare which has never before surfaced in a public place. The museum tells the story of 11 million of the world's citizens killed by the Nazis between 1933 and 1945. This is a story not of war, but of human nature itself gone berserk. In so far as possible, the victims and the survivors tell of their direct experience. As a visitor, I found myself horrified and shocked but compelled to continue, and grateful when provided with a place to rest and reflect. The Hall of Remembrance on the ground floor provides just such a space with filtered light and soaring stonework transforming the museum from historic monument to place of spiritual solace. The implicit question posed by the museum is not: Why did it happen?, but: How do we prevent similar occurrences? Thinking deeply about this question is perhaps the challenge of the visit.

HIGHLIGHTS

- Main exhibition
- Hall of Remembrance
- Hall of Witness
- Works of art
- For children over 12: *Daniel's Story*

INFORMATION

- ✚ G5
- ✉ 14th Street and Wallenberg Place SW. South of Independence
- ☎ 202/488 0400, Ticketmaster 202/432 SEAT, 800/551 SEAT
- 🕐 Daily 10–5:30
- 🍴 Kosher restaurant
- Ⓢ Smithsonian
- ♿ Excellent
- 🎫 Free
- ↔ Presidents' Memorials (➤ 26, 31, 32), Smithsonian Institution (➤ 36), Bureau of Engraving and Printing (➤ 35)
- ❓ Timed tickets distributed at 10AM daily; advance tickets through Ticketmaster 202/432 7328, 800/551 7328; queue early (before 9AM) or book two weeks in advance.

11

NATIONAL MUSEUM OF AMERICAN HISTORY

HIGHLIGHTS

- The Star Spangled Banner
- Statue of George Washington by Horatio Greenough
- Hands-on-History Room
- Hands-on-Science Room
- *John Bull*
- Muhammed Ali's boxing gloves
- Ruby slippers from *The Wizard of Oz*

INFORMATION

- ✚ G5
- ✉ Constitution Avenue and 14th Street NW
- ☎ 202/357 2700
- 🕐 Daily 10–5:30
- 🍽 Cafeteria
- Ⓜ Smithsonian, Federal Triangle
- ♿ Excellent
- 🎫 Free
- ↔ Smithsonian Institution (➤ 36), US Holocaust Memorial Museum (➤ 33), Bureau of Engraving and Printing (➤ 35)
- ❓ Tours available

❝Here is told the story of all the American people. From the Star Spangled Banner to Judy Garland's ruby slippers to Duke Ellington's papers to the gowns worn by First Ladies at inaugural balls, here are the objects which tell of life in America.❞

What to see The museum mounts exhibits depicting events and themes which define American life. Among these, 'Field to Factory' tells the story of African Americans migrating from the rural, agricultural South to northern industrial cities. 'A More Perfect Union' contributes to the on-going dialogue about the American Constitution by depicting the withdrawing of civil liberties from Japanese Americans during World War II. The largest exhibition ever mounted is 'The Information Age', rich in automated gear ranging from early telephones to robotics to high-definition television. 'From Parlor to Politics' and 'First Ladies: Political Role and Public Image' depict women's political impact. Big exhibits on the Industrial Revolution and 'Science in American Life' round out the offerings. Post your cards in the original West Virginia general store, get your picture taken in front of the 280-ton steam engine *John Bull*, the oldest working locomotive in the country and have an old-fashioned float in the ice cream parlour.

George Washington as a Greek god

BUREAU OF ENGRAVING & PRINTING

❝*Nondescript government buildings rarely attract the attention of tourists. Here at the Bureau of Engraving and Printing, however, children and adults alike take pleasure in watching the powerful printing presses turn out over $20 million per day .*❞

History The Bureau moved to this site back in 1930 from the red-brick Auditor's Building still standing on the corner, and prints all US currency, stamps, presidential invitations and military certificates. Federal presses produce a staggering $100 billion annually, in addition to 30 billion postage stamps. If the printing process goes even slightly awry and produces imperfect bills, the coveted greenbacks are summarily shredded. Also here is the grandly titled Office of Mutilated Currency, where citizens go to redeem bills partially destroyed by fire, flood, laundry mishaps or animals.

What to see Visitors see a film on the history of currency and file past processing rooms where over $20 million a day are produced. The printing room produces giant currency sheets, each holding 32 bills. The sheets are then trimmed, stacked and bundled for distribution to the Federal Reserve Banks across the nation. The self-guided, 20-minute tour ends at an exhibition hall which contains informative displays on the history of currency, counterfeiting and stamps.

Do not be daunted by the queues: they move rapidly. Outside, you'll find yourself near the Tidal Basin with its paddle boats and tree-lined pathways, strewn with petals from the cherry trees in early spring. This is one of the most beautiful sights the city has to offer.

HIGHLIGHTS

- View of the Tidal Basin
- Presses printing dollars
- Film on the history of currency
- Exhibition on stamps
- Stacks of money, bundled for shipping

INFORMATION

- ✚ G6
- ✉ 14 and C Streets SW
- ☎ 202/874 3188
- 🕐 All year, Mon–Fri 9–2. Closed 25 Dec
- Ⓜ Smithsonian
- ♿ Excellent
- 🎫 Free
- ↔ US Holocaust Memorial Museum (➤ 33)
- ❓ Self-guided tours. Tickets available during peak tourist seasons on Wallenberg Place

13

SMITHSONIAN INSTITUTION

INFORMATION

- ➕ G5/H5
- ✉ Jefferson Drive at 10th Street SW
- ☎ 202/357 2700
- ◷ Daily 9–5:30
- 🍴 The Commons for Smithsonian Members
- Ⓜ Smithsonian
- ♿ Excellent
- ✚ Free
- ❓ Film every 20 mins

"Tourists streaming off Metro escalators on a summer morning frequently ask briefcase-toting commuters, 'Where is the Smithsonian?' There is usually a suspicious silence when the local answers: 'Everything you see is the Smithsonian'."

History An Englishman, James Smithson, stipulated that his estate should go 'to the United States of America, to found at Washington, under the name of the Smithsonian Institution an Establishment for the increase and diffusion of knowledge...' After typical political wrangling, John Quincy Adams convinced Congress to accept the gift, which was worth about $515,000 when it was accepted in 1846. Today there are 15 museums and the national zoo, 140 million objects and specimens, countless research projects in almost every country on earth, 6,000 employees and an annual budget of nearly $400 million.

What to see Start your visit at James Renwick's 1855 turreted, asymmetrical, red-sandstone 'Castle', recently renovated into a visitor information centre. The Castle staff, mostly volunteers, are multilingual, as are many brochures, interactive maps and touch-screen programmes, all designed to assist visitors to the Smithsonian and to other Washington sights.

The different museums of the Institution are mainly on both sides of the Mall, between 3rd and 14th Streets. Research is conducted on Russian voles, Native American baskets, endangered insects of the rain forests, aerodynamics, molecular biology, metallurgy, linguistics, political science, ancient foodways, textile manufacture, and these topics are only the ones which come immediately to mind.

FBI Building

"*Americans are law-abiding citizens, but nothing fascinates them more than crime and crime prevention. The FBI Building is on most children's lists of 'ten most wanted' things to do in the District.***"**

History Stanley Gladych's modern, poured-concrete building in the New Brutalism school of architecture conjures Big Brother looming halfway between the Capitol and the White House on Pennsylvania Avenue. Eight thousand federal employees operate out of the city-block square which embodies the 'idea of a central core of files'. The FBI is the supreme federal authority on domestic crime, having grown from an investigative force chartered in 1908, and its wide-ranging remit includes terrorism, organised crime and industrial espionage among much else. Even today, the FBI is instilled with the values of its most famous leader, J Edgar Hoover, who ran the agency from 1928 to 1972, an astounding 44 years. FBI agents remain the most respected investigative force in America and their headquarters is one of the most popular tourist attractions in Washington: be prepared to queue.

What to see The tour consists of historical exhibits about famous cases the FBI has solved, an introduction to laboratory work including DNA analysis of hair fibres and blood samples, fingerprint matching and a live-ammunition firearms demonstration followed by a question and answer session. Be alert when you visit: two of the FBI's most-wanted characters were fingered by tourists who saw the 'Wanted' posters while on the tour.

HIGHLIGHTS

- Live-ammo demo
- FBI Most Wanted files
- FBI Most Famous Cases
- Exhibition of FBI history
- Insight into the lives and training of FBI agents

INFORMATION

- ✚ G5
- ✉ E and 10th Streets NW
- ☎ 202/324 3447
- 🕐 Mon–Fri 8:45–4:15
- Ⓜ Federal Triangle
- ♿ Excellent
- 🎟 Free
- ↔ Smithsonian Institution (► 36), Ford's Theatre (► 78)

FBI crest

15

AMERICAN ART & PORTRAIT GALLERIES

HIGHLIGHTS

The National Portrait Gallery
- *Thomas Jefferson* and *George and Martha Washington* by Gilbert Stuart
- Works by Mary Cassatt and John Singleton Copley
- Paintings of Native Americans by George Catlin
- Photographs of sports figures

The National Museum of American Art
- *The Spiral*, Alexander Calder
- *Throne of the Third Heaven of the Nations' Millennium General Assembly*, James Hampton
- Ash Can School paintings
- *The Chasm of the Colorado* and *The Grand Canyon of the Yellowstone*, Thomas Moran

INFORMATION

- ➕ H4
- ✉ Old Patent Office Building, 8th and F Streets NW
- ☎ 202/357 2700
- 🕐 Daily 10–5:30
- 🍴 Patent Pending
- Ⓖ Gallery Place
- ♿ Excellent
- 🆓 Free
- ↔ Friendship Arch (➤ 56)
- ❓ Mon–Fri 10, 3; Sun 11:15

"*These two museums off the National Mall are under-attended and more's the pity. Make the effort and you will find quiet galleries, wonderful collections of American art and intelligent history.***"**

History Two Smithsonian museums are housed in the 19th-century Greek-Revival Old Patent Office Building: the National Portrait Gallery and the National Museum of American Art.

National Portrait Gallery The National Portrait Gallery, in the southern part of the building, superbly blends history and art, providing a context for the intimate story told through the portrait sitters and their legacies. Here you will find the stories of prominent Colonial Americans, First Peoples, American artists, inventors, industrialists, educators, politicians and civic and military leaders. Exhibitions include aspects of portrait-painting and historical events.

George Washington from the collection of the National Portrait Gallery

National Museum of American Art The National Museum of American Art, in the northern part of the building, features American folk art galleries, portrayals of the American West, George Catlin's paintings of American Indians, American Impressionists, the Ash Can School painters and other noted Americans like John Singer Sargent, Thomas Eakins, Mary Cassatt, Romaine Brooks and pop artist Jasper Johns.

NATIONAL ARCHIVES

"We Americans have neither a monarchy nor state religion, but we do worship law. Nowhere is this worship more apparent than in the National Archives."

History Occupied in 1935, John Russell Pope's beaux-arts building serves as repository for the government's valuable documents. At the last count it contained 3.2 billion textual documents, 1.6 million maps, 14.9 million photographs and enough film and video to encircle the globe many times.

What to see After passing through a metal detector, visitors proceed reverently towards a throne-like structure in a domed rotunda with Corinthian columns and arched pediment. Raised at the centre of the structure are enshrined the Declaration of Independence, the Bill of Rights and the Constitution, sealed in bronze helium-filled cases covered with green ultra-violet filters. If you wanted actually to read the Charters of Freedom, as they are called, forget it. The conservation techniques employed make reading impossible, as does the steady stream of visitors patiently waiting their turn to cast their gaze upon the written, but no longer read, work. At the end of each day, after all the visitors and researchers have gone home, the security staff lower the throne and the Charters within into a bomb-proof vault beneath the exhibition floor for safe-keeping.

Also on exhibition are murals by Barry Faulkner entitled *The Declaration of Independence* and *The Constitution*. There is a changing exhibition space which shows material from the vast collections maintained by the Archives – everything from letters to photographs, to posters.

HIGHLIGHTS

- Charters of Freedom
- Magna Carta, on loan from Ross Perot
- Murals by Barry Faulkner
- Changing exhibition gallery

INFORMATION

- ✚ H5
- ✉ Constitution Avenue at 7th Street NW
- ☎ 202/501 5205
- 🕐 Daily 10–5:30
- Ⓠ Archives
- ♿ Excellent
- 🆓 Free
- ↔ Smithsonian Institution (➤ 36), US Capitol (➤ 43), US Botanic Gardens (➤ 42)
- ❓ Tours daily at 10:30 and 1:15 (reservations required)

17

NATIONAL GALLERY OF ART

HIGHLIGHTS

- East Wing
- Glass tetrahedrons in plaza
- *Knife Edge Mirror Two Pieces*, Henry Moore,
- Alexander Calder's mobile, East Wing atrium
- *Mercury surrounded by Tuscan marble colums*
- *The Alba Madonna*, Raphael
- *Venus and Adonis*, Titian
- *Daniel in the Lion's Den*, Rubens
- *Woman Holding a Balance*, Vermeer
- *The Skater*, Gilbert Stuart
- Waterwall visible from plaza and concourse

INFORMATION

- ✚ H5
- ✉ Madison Drive between 3rd and 7th Streets NW
- ☎ 202/737 4215
- ◷ Mon–Sat 10–5; Sun 11–6
- 🍴 Waterfall Cafeteria
- ▣ Archives
- ♿ Excellent
- 🔰 Free
- ↔ US Botanic Gardens (➤ 42), US Capitol (➤ 43), National Air and Space Museum (➤ 41)

"My first exposure to acres of fine art was a visit to the National Gallery of Art after an anti-Vietnam War march on Washington in 1969. Civic pride overcame me when I realised that every citizen owned an equal share of it."

History When Andrew Mellon was Secretary of the Treasury (1921–32), he realised that the capital city lacked a great gallery showing the development of western art. He determined to remedy this failing and when he died in 1937 he left an endowment, his renowned collection of paintings and sculpture, to the American people, and his dream to his son, Paul. Paul Mellon oversaw the construction of John Russell Pope's Classical-Revival building (opened in 1941) and, eventually, I M Pei's visually stunning East Wing, to my mind the most beautiful modern building in America, opened in 1978.

What to see The permanent collection begins with Italian Renaissance painting, including the Spanish painters Velasquez, El Greco and Goya as well as Flemish, German, and Dutch painting from van der Weyden and Dürer to Rubens and Vermeer. The French are abundantly represented by Watteau, Corot, Manet, Renoir, and all the pre-, neo- and post-Impressionists. Works by William Hogarth begin the tour of British painting which follows, from Gainsborough to Turner. The Americans, too, are widely represented by Gilbert Stuart, Winslow Homer, James McNeill Whistler, and many, many other contributors to the creative patrimony.

This pre-eminent museum also offers films, symposia and lectures on the collection, while the 'micro gallery' computerised collection brings the gallery right into the Information Age.

NATIONAL AIR & SPACE MUSEUM

"Why is the National Air and Space Museum the most visited museum in the world? Imagination. This museum allows parents and children alike to extend to the edges of imagination."

History This museum was the Smithsonian's bicentennial gift to the nation, opening in 1976. It houses a collection begun as early as 1861, when the first Secretary of the Smithsonian encouraged experiments in balloon flight. Today the collection includes the Wright Brothers' 1903 *Flyer*, Charles Lindbergh's *Spirit of St Louis*, Chuck Yeager's *Bell X-1*, in which he broke the sound barrier, and *The Voyager* in which Dick Rutan and Jeana Yeager flew non-stop around the world.

What to see In the Space Halls stand the Columbia Space Shuttle, Apollo-Soyuz spacecraft, Skylab and Lunar Exploration Vehicles, to name but a few of the spectacular rockets, missiles and space vehicles on view. Also here, and at the centre of on-going controversy over the events leading to the end of World War II, is the *Enola Gay*, the plane that carried the atomic bomb dropped on Hiroshima, Japan.

HIGHLIGHTS

- Wright Brothers' 1903 *Flyer*
- Charles Lindbergh's *Spirit of St Louis*
- Chuck Yeager's *Bell X-1 Glamorous Glennis*
- John Glenn's *Friendship* and *Apollo 11*
- Soviet 'Sputnik'
- Vertical Flight Gallery
- Lunar Exploration Vehicles
- Amelia Earhart's Lockheed Vega 5B

INFORMATION

- ✚ H5
- ✉ Independence Avenue at 6th Street SW
- ☎ 202/357 2700
- ⏰ Daily 10–5:30
- 🍴 Wright Place, cafeteria
- Ⓜ L'Enfant Plaza
- ♿ Excellent
- 🎫 Free
- ↔ US Botanic Gardens (► 42), National Gallery of Art (► 40)

Spirit of St Louis, *flown by Charles Lindbergh*

US BOTANIC GARDENS

HIGHLIGHTS

- Seasonal displays
- Cactus House
- Orchids and tropical plants
- Coffee, chocolate and banyan trees
- Bartholdi Fountain

INFORMATION

- H5
- 1st Street SW
- 202/225 7099
- Daily 9–5
- Federal Center SW
- Excellent
- Free
- Smithsonian Institution (➤ 36), US Capitol (➤ 43)

❝*The poinsettia display at the US Botanic Gardens in December is an annual holiday event for many Washington families. I like to visit during a weekday winter morning when, alone in the desert display, I can easily imagine a strong sun and a dry breeze.*❞

History US explorers needed a place to conserve specimens from the South Seas, and Congress authorised the first greenhouse in 1842. The present 40,000-square-foot conservatory, an attractive combination of iron-and-glass greenhouse and stone orangeries, was erected in 1931 at the southwestern corner of Capitol Hill.

What to see The entrance hall serves as a seasonal gallery where the visitor may encounter Christmas poinsettias, spring tulips and hyacinths, or autumn chrysanthemums. Orchids are always on display. There is a permanent planting of high desert flora as well as a steamy tropical exhibit.

Experienced city-goers, with the ability to ignore traffic whizzing by, appreciate the tiny pocket park across Independence Avenue, arguably the most beautiful in the city. The plantings frame and showcase the cast-iron Bartholdi Fountain, embellished with sea nymphs, monsters, tritons and lighted globes, which dates from 1876. Frédéric-Auguste Bartholdi is best known in the US as the sculptor of the Statue of Liberty, a French gift to the people of America. He designed this fountain for the Philadelphia Centennial Exhibition, intending it to represent the elements of light and water. Picnics can be held at the tables on the Summer Terrace.

US CAPITOL

❝The dome of the US Capitol is a familiar backdrop for television newscasters and politicians attempting to associate their pronouncements with this unrivalled symbol of American democracy.❞

History The dome was an engineering feat when undertaken in 1851 by Capitol architect Charles Walter and Army Quartermaster General Montgomery Meigs. It became a political symbol before it was half finished; Civil War broke out and the Capitol housed the wounded and their care-givers. Many advised President Lincoln to halt construction, as happened to government projects such as the Washington Monument, but he was adamant that work on the dome be taken as 'a sign we intend the Union shall go on'. The 9-million-pound, cast-iron dome rises 280 feet.

What to see Visitors first encounter the Great Rotunda created by the dome. You may wait here for a guide or wander freely alone in the public spaces. The large paintings hung overhead, depicting scenes of George Washington's leadership, were painted from life and memory by his aide, John Trumbull. *The Apotheosis of Washington*, a fresco by Italian immigrant Constantino Brumidi, fills the ceiling with classical deities and the Founding Fathers. Brumidi, it was said at the time, consorted with 'ladies of the night', whose likenesses then appeared as ample maidens ministering to George Washington at the very pinnacle of American power: the Capitol dome.

HIGHLIGHTS

- Rotunda
- Frescos by Constantino Brumidi
- 10-ton bronze Columbus Doors
- Statuary Hall
- Old Senate Chamber

INFORMATION

- ✚ J5
- ✉ 1st Street between Independence and Constitution Avenues
- ☎ 202/225 6827
- 🕐 Daily, 9–3:45
- 🍴 Capitol Cafeteria, Dining Room
- Ⓜ Capitol South
- ♿ Excellent
- 🎫 Free
- ↔ Union Station (➤ 44), US Botanic Gardens(➤ 42), Library of Congress (➤ 46), Supreme Court (➤ 45)
- ❓ Tours daily, every 15 mins. A pass to observe a session of Congress can be obtained from a senator's or representative's office by US nationals. Foreign visitors apply at the ground floor appointment desk. When Congress works overtime, the exterior dome light in the cupola is lit and visitors are welcome on a first come, first served basis.

The dome's colonnade   43

21

UNION STATION

HIGHLIGHTS

- Main Hall
- Statues of Roman legionnaires
- East Hall
- Presidential Waiting Room
- Columbus Plaza

INFORMATION

- J4
- 40 Massachusetts Avenue NE
- 202/371 9441
- 24 hours for train service; shops, restaurants and theatres vary
- Many, for all budgets
- Union Station
- Excellent
- Free
- US Capitol and Capitol Hill attractions (➤ 43)

"Union Station is a public treasure for all people: movie-going teenagers, professional women shopping at lunch, dining deal-makers, commuting bureaucrats and tourists taking in the sights."

History Architect Daniel H Burnham lived up to his motto 'make no little plans' when he undertook the consolidation of the District's several train lines early this century. Burnham's beaux-arts, white-marble, vaulted Union Station was the largest train station in the world when it opened in 1907.

Completely renovated and reopened in 1988, today's Union Station includes restaurants for every budget, nine cinema screens and sophisticated boutique shopping, as well as serving as an active train terminal and Metro stop.

What to see The exterior allegorical neo-classical sculptures of fire, electricity and mechanics set off the skyline and a grand memorial to Christopher Columbus by Lorado Taft fronts the massive Doric colonnade.

Travellers by the thousand pass under the cavernous 96-foot-high coffered, gold-leaf embellished ceiling, guarded patiently by 46 statues of Roman legionnaires by sculptor Augustus Saint-Gaudens. The original Presidential Waiting Room is now a restaurant.

When you walk outside, to the right you can visit another recently restored Burnham building: the Old Post Office, which now houses the Smithsonian Postal Museum. And to the left you can see contemporary beaux-arts styling in the new Thurgood Marshall Federal Judicial Center by Edward Larrabee Barnes.

SUPREME COURT BUILDING

"*One of the justices called this 1935 neo-classical gleaming Vermont marble building, designed by Cass Gilbert Jr, 'bombastically pretentious ... for a quiet group of old boys such as the Supreme Court'.***"**

History Well, the Court is no longer an old boys' ghetto, with Justices Sandra Day O'Conner and Ruth Bader Ginsburg, and, in fact, it has never been really quiet. The 1857 *Dred Scott* decision holding that Congress had no authority to limit slavery contributed to the onset of the Civil War. Rulings on abortion have frequently made the wide open court plaza a focus of civil disobedience. *Brown v. Board of Education* required integration of schools and bussing across the land, and *Engel v. Vitale* outlawed school prayer.

But, in another way, the Court does work quietly. The justices are appointed for life and rarely give interviews. The Court is not televised and, unlike the rest of Washington, leaks of information never percolate out of this staid edifice.

What to see When the Court is in session (Oct–Jun), casual visitors can spend a few minutes viewing the workings of the Court by waiting in the 'three minute line'. There is a small exhibition on court history, and the building itself, one of Washington's most impressive Greek temples, is certainly worth the time. The magnificent bronze entrance doors, designed by John Donnely Jr, and weighing 13 tons, depict the world's legal systems. Inside, sculpted friezes by James Earle Frazier show *The Contemplation of Justice and The Authority of Law*.

HIGHLIGHTS

- Bronze entrance doors
- Plaza sculpture
- Busts of chief justices
- Film and exhibits on court history
- Statue of Justice John Marshall
- The Court in session

INFORMATION

- ✚ J5
- ✉ 1st and East Capitol Streets NE
- ☎ 202/479 3211
- ◷ Mon–Fri 9–4:30
- 🍴 Cafeteria
- Ⓒ Capitol South, Union Station
- ♿ Excellent
- 💲 Free
- ↔ Library of Congress (► 46), US Capitol (► 43)
- ❓ Lectures on the half-hour when the Court is not in session

Spring blossom softens the stern façade

23

LIBRARY OF CONGRESS

HIGHLIGHTS

- Neptune Fountain by Roland Hinton Perry
- 'Torch of Learning' on green copper dome
- Great Hall
- Main Reading Room
- Stained glass, arched windows
- Sculpture inside and out
- View of the Capitol from the Madison Building cafeteria

INFORMATION

- ✚ J5
- ✉ 1st Street and Independence Avenue SE
- ☎ 202/707 5458
- ◷ Mon–Fri 9–9; Sat 9–5:30
- 🍴 Cafeteria
- Ⓠ Capitol South
- ♿ Excellent. Visitor Services (☎ 202/707 9779) provides American Sign Language interpretation. TTY 202/7076362
- 🔄 Free
- ↔ US Capitol (▶ 43), Supreme Court (▶ 45)
- ❓ Tours Mon–Fri 10:30, 11:30, 1:30, 3:30. Library resources are open to any individual 18 years or older pursuing research

The copper dome and Torch of Learning

❝*When asked about the advantages of living in Washington, many residents list the libraries. Chief among these is the Library of Congress.*❞

History As early as 1800, Congress appropriated funds for a library. Unfortunately, when the British sacked the Capitol in 1814 they destroyed the library. Thomas Jefferson's personal library then became the nucleus of the new collection. The granite beaux-arts Jefferson Building demands attention through a ceremonial portico, carved balustrades, Corinthian columns, massive quoins and sculpted busts of men of letters gazing down on the passing scene. The Main Reading Room serves as a scholarly mecca. Sitting at the mahogany readers' tables 160 feet below the domed ceiling is an experience of an almost spiritual nature for many researchers.

What to see Today, more than 100 million items fill 600 miles of shelves in the Jefferson, Madison and Adams buildings, clustered between 1st and 3rd Streets on Pennsylvania Avenue SE. Holdings include the largest map collection in the world, a Gutenberg Bible, Jefferson's first version of the Declaration of Independence, Lincoln's drafts of the Emancipation Proclamation and the Gettysburg Address, Stradivarius violins, the various contents of Lincoln's pockets on the evening he was shot, original scores by both Brahms and Beethoven, and props and papers belonging to Houdini.

SHRINE OF THE IMMACULATE CONCEPTION

American Catholic: big, ordered, crisp. These adjectives describe the National Shrine of the Immaculate Conception dedicated to Christ's mother, Mary, named Patroness of the United States by Pope Pius IX in 1847.

History Work began in the grounds of the Catholic University in 1920. In 1926 the Crypt Church was complete. After the Great Depression and World War II construction began again in earnest during 1954. Completed with characteristic American efficiency, the Great Upper Church was dedicated on 20 November 1959.

What to see Separating the Crypt Church from the Chapel of Our Lady of Hostyn is a supremely delicate stained-glass screen depicting scenes from the life of Saint John Neumann, the first American man to have been canonised.

The Byzantine-style dome (237 feet in height and 108 feet in diameter) is lavishly decorated with Marian symbols in gold-leaf and coloured tiles. The 329-foot-high bell tower houses a 56-bell carillon cast in France and supports a 20-foot gilded cross visible for miles around in every direction.

Three rose windows embellished with gold and amethyst illuminate the sanctuary, along with ranks of other windows depicting the lives of Mary, the Holy Family, saints and redeemed sinners. But the lasting image visitors take away is that of the extraordinary mosaics, acres of them on ceilings and walls, in the apse and in chapels, donated by American Catholics of all ethnic origins.

HIGHLIGHTS

- Ecclesiastical sculpture
- Mosaics

INFORMATION

- ✚ Off map, north of K1
- ✉ 4th Street and Michigan Avenue NE
- ☎ 202/526 8300
- ⏰ Apr–Oct 7–7; Nov–Mar 7–6
- 🍴 Cafeteria daily 7:30–2:30
- Ⓜ Brookland
- ♿ Excellent
- 🎫 Free
- ❓ Tours by appointment, Mon–Sat 9–12, 1–3; Sun 1:30–3

The Byzantine-style Christ in the dome

47

25

CEDAR HILL

HIGHLIGHTS

- Harriet Beecher Stowe's desk
- Rocking chair, gift of Republic of Haiti
- 1,000-volume library
- Portraits of Elizabeth Cady Stanton and Susan B Anthony
- View of Washington

INFORMATION

- ✚ L8
- ✉ 1411 W Street SE
- ☎ 202/426 5961
- 🕐 Daily 9–5. Closed 25 Dec, 1 Jan
- 🚌 By Tourmobile
- ☎ 202/554 7950.
- **By car**: 11th Street Bridge to Martin Luther King Avenue, left on W Street
- ♿ Good
- 🎫 Free
- ❓ One-hour tours given on the half hour

Statue of Frederick Douglass

❝*When historic houses hold the decorative arts, libraries and family mementoes of the previous occupants, they can provide the intimacy of a personal visit. Cedar Hill, home of America's famous abolitionist Frederick Douglass, is such a place.***❞**

History Douglass, christened Frederick Augustus Washington Bailey about 1818, wrote that when his mother died seven years later he had never seen her in the daylight. He had been separated from her at birth by a distance of 12 miles, a distance she infrequently walked after work, leaving a few hours later to be back in the fields by sun up. Despite this humble beginning, Douglass learned the ship-caulker's trade, escaped to Paris to avoid slave bounty hunters, lectured widely and published on anti-slavery, became an advisor to President Lincoln, an ambassador to Haiti, and a staunch supporter of women's suffrage. When he moved into the Italianate-style Cedar Hill he was the first black resident of Anacostia, breaking the prohibition against 'Irish, Negro, mulatto, or persons of African blood'.

What to see Cedar Hill, now The Frederick Douglass National Historic Site, occupies the highest point in Anacostia, with a great view of the Anacostia River and the capital city. The property is now operated by the National Park Service, which provides an information centre and a book store specialising in African American titles.

Among the many artefacts on display inside the house are the desk at which Harriet Beecher Stowe wrote *Uncle Tom's Cabin*, and the 1,000 volumes of Douglass's original library.

WASHINGTON's *best*

49

AFRICAN AMERICAN SITES

1212 T Street NW, the house where 'Duke' Ellington grew up in the early 1900s

Lincoln Theatre

Opened in 1922 as a first-run movie theatre which catered for black patrons who were either barred from white theatres or forced to sit in the balcony, the theatre has recently been restored to its original condition and now serves for performances of all kinds, contributing to the rejuvenation of the U Street corridor, once widely known as 'Black Broadway'.

➕ G2 ✉ 1215 U Street NW
☎ 202/328 6000
🕐 Open for performances
50 🚇 U Street–Cardozo

See Top 25 Sights for
CEDAR HILL (►48)
LINCOLN MEMORIAL (►26)

ANACOSTIA MUSEUM

This Smithsonian museum depicts African American art and heritage through changing exhibitions and public programmes which attract neighbourhood residents and visitors from the four corners of the globe.

➕ M9 ✉ 1901 Fort Place SE ☎ 202/287 3369 🕐 Daily 10–5
♿ Daily free bus service available from the Smithsonian Castle 🎟 Free

EDWARD KENNEDY 'DUKE' ELLINGTON RESIDENCE

Though born at 1217 22nd Street NW, Duke Ellington (1899–1974, ► 12) grew up on this street, taking piano lessons nearby. He first appeared with his band, *Duke's Serenaders*, at True Reformers Hall, a local dance spot on U Street. By 1931, he was being described as 'the biggest inspiration we had ... the epitome of what we wanted to be', following his performance at the gala reopening of the Howard Theater.

➕ G2 ✉ 1212 T Street NW 🕐 Not open to the public
🚇 U Street–Cardozo

FATHER PATRICK FRANCIS HEALY BUILDING, GEORGETOWN UNIVERSITY

This 1879 baronial fantasy dominating Georgetown University's Potomac riverfront honours the first black Catholic priest and bishop in America, who later became president of Georgetown University.

➕ C3 ✉ 37th and O Streets NW ☎ 202/687 5055 🕐 24 hours

FREDERICK DOUGLASS HOUSE

This Victorian townhouse with mansard roof was the first Washington home of one of the country's most famous abolitionists. It later housed the National Museum of African Art, now part of the Smithsonian museums.

➕ K5 ✉ 316 A Street NE 🕐 Not open to the public 🚇 Capitol South

HOWARD UNIVERSITY

Chartered in 1867 to educate freed men and women, Howard's neo-colonial, neo-Georgian and modern buildings on 89 acres today house 12,000 students pursuing nearly 200 areas of study. Howard Law School is widely acknowledged as the place where African Americans learned the legal system which they later used to drive the Civil Rights Movement of the 1960s. Thurgood Marshall, associate justice of the Supreme Court, was a Howard graduate.

✚ H2 ✉ 2400 6th Street NW 20059 ☎ 202/806 6100
🕐 Mon–Fri 9–5 🚇 Shaw–Howard University

INDUSTRIAL BANK OF WASHINGTON

Blacks could deposit money in white banks, but the banks would not lend to black homeowners or entrepreneurs. When John L Lewis opened his bank on this spot in 1913 it soon became known as 'the wage earners' bank'. In 1932 Texan Jesse Mitchell opened Industrial on this site with $200,000; the bank continues to serve Washington's African American community.

✚ G2 ✉ 2000 11th Street NW ☎ 202/722 2050 🕐 Mon–Fri 9–3; Fri 4:30–6; Sat Drive-In 9–noon 🚇 U Street–Cardozo

LINCOLN PARK

Charlotte Scott, a Virginian woman, contributed the first $5 toward the Emancipation Memorial, which was supported entirely from funds from free blacks. The memorial was dedicated on 14 April 1876 and remained the city's only monument to Lincoln until 1922, when the Lincoln Memorial was dedicated. In 1974, the Emancipation Memorial was turned away from the Capitol, toward the newly erected memorial to Mary McLeod Bethune (► 12).

✚ K5 ✉ East Capitol Street between 11th and 13th Streets 🚇 Eastern Market

TRUE REFORMERS HALL

This six-storey 1903 building housed a variety of black-owned retail stores, entertainments, offices, and a drill room and armoury for Washington's black national guard unit. The United Order of True Reformers awarded architect John A Lankford his first major commission with this building. It later housed a popular dance hall, where 'Duke' Ellington performed (► 12 and 50), and the Metropolitan Police Boys Club for black children.

✚ G2 ✉ 1200 U Street NW 🚇 U Street–Cardozo

Black Broadway

Since the 1968 riots sparked by the assassination of Martin Luther King, Jr, U Street NW, near the U Street–Cardozo Metro, has undergone a transformation. With the reopening in 1994 of the 1,250-seat Lincoln Theatre, the strip once again deserves the appellation 'Black Broadway'. Community Rhythms, the vibrant murals of artist Al Smith, decorate the Metro entrances and depict the area's renaissance.

Mary McLeod Bethune Memorial, Lincoln Park

MARY McLEOD BETHUNE
1875 1955
Let her works praise her

51

FOR CHILDREN

See Top 25 Sights for
BUREAU OF ENGRAVING AND PRINTING (▶35)
FBI BUILDING (▶37)
NATIONAL GEOGRAPHIC SOCIETY, EXPLORERS
    HALL (▶29)
UNION STATION (▶44)

Information Sources

The Washington Post 'Carousel Weekend' lists up-to-the-moment events for children. WKDL radio (1050 AM) caters for children and their parents, and often reports on children's events.

THE SMITHSONIAN MUSEUMS

These museums entertain and educate millions of children every year about everything from aardvarks and aeroplanes to singing insects and space suits. Of special interest are the dinosaurs and the insect zoo at the National Museum of Natural History (➕ G5 ✉ Constitution Avenue and 12th Street NW); the Hands-on-History and Hands-on-Science rooms at the National Museum of American History (▶ 34); 'Amazonia' and the Invertebrate House at the National Zoological Park (▶ 53); the IMAX films at the National Air and Space Museum (▶ 41); and Discovery Theater (➕ G5 ✉ 900 Jefferson Drive SW ☎ 202/357 1500) where puppet shows, plays and storytelling are held. ☎ 202/357 2700 .

CAPITAL CHILDREN'S MUSEUM

Everything is messy here, as if a horde of happy children had played with everything in the place for years, and they have. Permanent exhibitions explore the cultures of Mexico and Thailand, animation, drawing from life and children's art, and children's health and well-being.
➕ J4 ✉ 800 3rd Street NE ☎ 202/543 8600 🕐 Daily 10–5 🚇 6 🚉 Union Station 💲 Cheap

HARD ROCK CAFÉ

A restaurant and a world-wide happening complete with T-shirts and baseball caps. Kids and their parents love the up-beat rock'n'roll hall of fame atmosphere and good-sized portions.
➕ G4 ✉ 999 E Street NW ☎ 202/737 7625 🕐 Weekdays 11–midnight; weekends 11AM–1AM 🚉 Metro Center

The National Museum of American History

METRO

Kids love the underground Metro system. Parents should be aware that Washingtonians use the escalators as urban exercise machines, so stand right, walk left. No eating, drinking, or smoking in Metro and, please, warn children that fingers and shoe laces can become caught in moving escalator parts.

NATIONAL AQUARIUM

Opened in 1873, the aquarium attracts youngsters with a popular touch-tank, sea turtles, moray eels and tropical and freshwater fish. Two o'clock shark and piranha feedings take place on alternate days.

⊞ G5 ⊠ 14th Street and Pennsylvania Avenue NW ☎ 202/482 2825 ⏰ Daily 9–5 Ⓜ Federal Triangle 💲 Cheap

NATIONAL ZOOLOGICAL PARK

Within the 160 acres landscaped by Frederick Law Olmsted Sr in 1889, zoo designers have constantly renovated enclosures to provide natural settings for birds, hoofed stock, komodo dragons, pygmy hippopotami, big cats, monkeys and much more. The Invertebrate House provides quiet for children to enjoy animals rarely seen.

⊞ E1 ⊠ 3001 Connecticut Avenue NW ☎ 202/673 4717 ⏰ Grounds: 15 Apr–15 Oct, 8–8; 16 Oct–14 Apr, 8–6; Animal Buildings 9–4:30; 'Amazonia' 10–4 🍴 Snack bars Ⓜ Woodley Park–Zoo 💲 Free

NAVY MUSEUM

Big, showy ships, cannons, missiles and submarines are scattered around the grounds and provide plenty of opportunities to peer through periscopes and pretend to conquer the seven seas.

⊞ K7 ⊠ 9th and M Streets SE, Building 76 ☎ 202/433 4882 ⏰ Weekdays 9–4; weekends and holidays 10–5 Ⓜ Eastern Market, Navy Yard 💲 Free

PLANET HOLLYWOOD

Owned by movie stars including Sylvester Stallone and Bruce Willis and decorated with cinema memorabilia, this restaurant specialises in burgers, pizzas, pasta and other American favourites including a merchandising arm with everything from caps to jackets.

⊞ G5 ⊠ 1101 Pennsylvania Avenue NW ☎ 202/783 7827 ⏰ Daily, 11AM–midnight Ⓜ Federal Triangle

PUPPET COMPANY PLAYHOUSE

Located in Glen Echo Park, MD, this troupe presents plays beloved by children of all ages.

⊞ Off map ⊠ 7300 MacArthur Boulevard, Glen Echo, MD ☎ 301/320 6668 💲 Free annual puppet exhibition; tickets cheap

SHOPPING FOR KIDS

FAO Schwarz stocks the best (or at least the most expensive) toys, dolls, children's books, and much more.

⊞ D3 ⊠ 3222 M Street NW ☎ 202/342 2285 ⏰ Mon–Sat 10–9; Sun 12–6 🍴 Café

The Kid's Closet sells baby clothes and gifts.

⊞ F3 ⊠ 1226 Connecticut Avenue NW ☎ 202/429 9247 ⏰ Mon–Fri 10–6; Sat 11–5 Ⓜ Dupont Circle

WASHINGTON DOLLS' HOUSE AND TOY MUSEUM

This museum is for looking at, not touching, an extensive collection of Victorian dolls, dolls' houses, toys and games.

⊞ Off map at D1 ⊠ 5236 44th Street NW ☎ 202/244 0024 ⏰ Tue–Sat 10–5; Sun noon–5 Ⓜ Friendship Heights 💲 Cheap

Tigers and other endangered species are bred at Washington's National Zoological Park

Babysitters

For sitters, check with the hotel concierge or call:

Chevy Chase Babysitters
⊠ 10771 Middleboro Drive, Damascus, MD 20872
☎ 301/916 2694

Helpers Plus Inc
⊠ 4700 Auth Place, Suite 401, Camp Springs, MD 20746
☎ 301/894 7200

Mothers' Aides Inc
⊠ Box 7088, Fairfax Station, VA 22039 ☎ 703/250 0700

WeeSit
⊠ 10681 Oak Thrust Court, Burke, VA 22015 ☎ 703/764 1542

LIBRARIES & ARCHIVES

See Top 25 Sights for
LIBRARY OF CONGRESS (►46)
NATIONAL ARCHIVES (►39)

A bookworm's paradise

When listing the reasons to live inside the Capital Beltway, many Washingtonians praise the literary scene. Museums and historic sites have acres of bookshelves crammed with publications relating to the museum collection and historic events and most have libraries open to researchers. Throughout the city, specialised collections are open to scholars and students of everything from Jewish American military history to Shakespeare.

BETHUNE MUSEUM AND ARCHIVES

Located in a Victorian townhouse near historic and architecturally interesting Logan Circle, this site is dedicated to preserving and documenting black women's participation in American history. Mary McLeod Bethune, political activist, educator and founder of the National Council of Negro Women, lived in this house, which also served as the headquarters of the Council.

✚ G3 ✉ 1318 Vermont Avenue NW ☎ 202/332 1233
🕐 Mon–Fri 10–4, Jun–Aug Sat 10–4 🚇 U Street–Cardozo, McPherson Square

FOLGER SHAKESPEARE LIBRARY

The world's most comprehensive collection of Shakespeare's works is included in this collection of 275,000 books and manuscripts from and about the European Renaissance. Collections are made available to scholars by appointment.

✚ J5 ✉ 201 E Capitol, SE ☎ 202/544 4600 🕐 Open to researchers Mon–Fri 10–4 🚇 Capitol South

HISTORICAL SOCIETY OF WASHINGTON

The Historical Society of Washington houses text and image collections relating to the social history of the District of Columbia. It is located in the ornate Victorian Heurich Mansion, built by a wealthy brewer.

✚ F3 ✉ 1307 New Hampshire Avenue NW ☎ 202/785 2068
🕐 Wed–Sat noon–3 🚇 Dupont Circle 💲 Cheap

MARTIN LUTHER KING MEMORIAL LIBRARY

The large, active, urban, main branch of the DC public library system, MLK has an extensive Washingtoniana collection as well as a Black Studies Division. Mies van der Rohe designed this unadorned steel and glass building, which opened in 1972 and is softened by Don Miller's mural celebrating the life of Martin Luther King Jr.

✚ G4 ✉ 901 G Street NW ☎ 202/727 1111 🕐 Mon–Thu 9–9; Fri–Sat 9–5:30 🚇 Gallery Place

MOORLAND-SPINGARN RESEARCH CENTER

Housed in the historic Founders Hall of Howard University, the Center includes extensive archives and secondary material about the African diaspora. All researchers are welcome in this non-circulating library.

✚ H2 ✉ 500 Howard Place in Founders Library, Howard University
☎ 202/806 7239 🕐 Mon–Fri 9–4:45 🚇 Shaw/Howard University

NATIONAL GEOGRAPHIC SOCIETY LIBRARY

This little-known library houses 50,000 books on geography, natural history, travel and topics which have long interested the Society, such as polar exploration. Of course all of the Society's publications, including a complete run of the famous yellow-spined magazine begun in 1888, are available. The reading room is well appointed with automated catalogue, good light and warm wood panelling.
➕ F3 ⊠ 17th and M Streets NW ☎ 202/857 7783 🕐 Mon–Fri 1:30–5 🚇 Dupont Circle, Farragut North

SMITHSONIAN INSTITUTION LIBRARIES

Smithsonian museums all have libraries open by appointment to researchers, from schoolchild to scholar. Collections include images of aeroplanes of all periods, world-wide biological flora and fauna, space, film and television, linguistics, palaeobiology, the history of rail transport, women's political life, domestic industry, war, peace, and everything in between. Of special note are the Archives of American Art, the National Anthropological Archives, and the Human Studies Film Archives.
☎ 202/357 1300

SUMNER SCHOOL MUSEUM AND ARCHIVES

Architect Adolph Cluss won a 'Medal for Progress' at the Vienna World's Exposition in 1873 for his innovative use of hallways and closets to shield classrooms from exterior noise. The school stood as a model example of black education during segregation and today houses the archives of the DC Public Schools.
➕ F3 ⊠ 17th and M Streets NW ☎ 202/727 3419 🕐 Tue–Sat 10–5 🚇 Dupont Circle

National Council of Negro Women

The Mary McLeod Bethune Museum and Archives house the records of the National Council of Negro Women, founded in 1935 and uniting the considerable influence of hundreds of African American women's groups. These women shaped public policy regarding civil rights, health care, housing and employment, extending even to the formation of the United Nations.

National Geographic Society

Outdoor Spaces
GARDENS, SCULPTURE & MEN ON HORSES

Washington summers can be sticky-hot but do not let the heat deter you from an exploration of the often inspiring, often whimsical sculptural placements, many with lovely gardens and plenty of shade.

Friendship Arch

Located at the Chinatown Metro, this gilded arch symbolises the energy and vitality of Washington's Asian community.

✚ H4 ✉ Chinatown, 7th and G Streets NW 🕐 24 hours 🚇 Gallery Place–Chinatown 🎟 Free

See Top 25 Sights for
BARTHOLDI FOUNTAIN AT THE US BOTANIC GARDENS (►42)
COLUMBUS PLAZA AT UNION STATION (►44)
JEFFERSON MEMORIAL (►32)
LINCOLN MEMORIAL (►26)
NEPTUNE'S COURT AT THE LIBRARY OF CONGRESS (►46)
VIETNAM VETERANS MEMORIAL AND CONSTITUTION GARDENS (►28)
WASHINGTON MONUMENT (►31)

THE AWAKENING

The Awakening, by J Seward Johnson, was installed as part of a temporary outdoor exhibition. So many Washingtonians, especially children, appreciated the bearded aluminium giant rising from the tip of Hains Point that it was retained by popular demand. The park in which it is set offers jogging and cycling paths, tennis, swimming, flowering cherry trees and a golf driving range.

✚ H9 ✉ Hains Point, East Potomac Park ☎ 202/485 9880, 202/727 6523 🕐 24 hours 🎟 Free

BISHOPS GARDEN

In total, there are 57 acres at Washington National Cathedral, tended by the All Hallows Guild, which hosts an annual flower show to raise funds for the gardens. The jewel in this crown is the Bishops Garden, which is designed around European ruins and a statue of the Prodigal Son. Plantings include herbs, boxwood, magnolia trees and tea roses.

✚ C1/D1 ✉ Wisconsin and Massachusetts Avenues NW ☎ 202/537 6200 🕐 May–Labor Day: Mon–Fri 10–9, Sat and Sun 10–4:30; Labor Day–30 April: daily 10–4:30 🚇 Tenley Town; 30 series bus south 🎟 Free

DUMBARTON OAKS

In 1944 the international conference leading to the formation of the United Nations was held at this estate, also known for its fine 10-acre formal garden.

✚ D2 ✉ 31st and R Streets NW ☎ 202/338 8278 🕐 Daily 2–5 🎟 Cheap

EINSTEIN MEMORIAL

Nestled in the grounds of one of Washington's most staid and august organisations, the National Academy of Sciences, is Robert Berks's whimsical sculpture of the physicist Albert Einstein, gently feeding the birds and inviting generations of children to sit on his lap.

➕ E5 ✉ 22nd Street NW and Constitution Avenue, in the grounds of the National Academy of Sciences ⏰ 24 hours 🚇 Foggy Bottom 🎫 Free

GRANT MEMORIAL

General Grant looks somewhat weary from the weight of his struggles as he sits on horseback at the foot of Capitol Hill. Animated artillery and cavalry flank Grant and create the most effective sculptural group in this city of men on horses.

➕ H5 ✉ 1st Street NW at the foot of Capitol Hill ⏰ 24 hours 🚇 Capitol South 🎫 Free

HILLWOOD MUSEUM

Appropriately, Hillwood graces Linnean Avenue, named after the Swedish naturalist who established naming conventions for the natural world. The grounds feature Buckingham Palace ivy, azaleas and rhododendrons, and 5,000 blooming orchids in the greenhouse.

➕ Off map ✉ 4155 Linnean Avenue NW ☎ 202/686 5807 ⏰ Tue–Sat 11–4:30 🍴 Tea Room Café 🚇 Van Ness–UDC 🎫 Moderate

HIRSHHORN SCULPTURE GARDEN

For a quiet and welcome respite from the cultural intensity of the National Mall, why not call in at this walled, sunken garden which boasts works by such luminaries as Henry Moore, Max Ernst, Pablo Picasso and Man Ray?

➕ H5 ✉ 7th Street and Jefferson Drive SW ☎ 202/357 2700 ⏰ 7:30–dusk 🚇 L'Enfant Plaza 🎫 Free

NATIONAL ARBORETUM

The Arboretum's 444 acres invite driving, cycling, hiking and even roller-blading. The Herbarium maintains 500,000 dried plants for research purposes, the azalea walk is a spring favourite, and the National Herb Garden and National Bonsai Collection are each a mecca for serious gardeners and general visitors alike.

➕ M3/N3 ✉ 3501 New York Avenue NE ☎ 202/245 2726 ⏰ Weekdays 8–5; weekends 10–5 🎫 Free

ROCK CREEK PARK

Washingtonians enjoy the 1,800 acres of Rock Creek Park as a counter-weight to the concrete, asphalt and marble found everywhere else in the city. Picnicking, cycling, hiking, tennis, golf and riding may all be enjoyed. The Nature Center and Planetarium have a full annual schedule.

➕ E1/E2/E3 ✉ Nature Center, 5000 Glover Road NW ☎ 202/426 6829 ⏰ Nature Center: Memorial Day–Labor Day, daily 9–5; Labor Day–Memorial Day, Wed–Sun 9–5; grounds: daylight hours 🚇 Woodley Park–Zoo 🎫 Free

Grant Memorial below Capitol Hill

Korean War Veterans Memorial

Dedicated in 1995, this memorial includes 19 life-size figures marching up an incline towards the American flag, a still pool memorialising those who lost their lives in the war and photographs of the Korean conflict etched into a 60-foot wall. This memorial of faces serves as a compelling counterpoint to the wall of names of the Vietnam Veterans Memorial.

➕ E5 ✉ Between the Lincoln Memorial and Independence Avenue ☎ 202/208 3561 ⏰ 24 hours 🎫 Free

PLACES TO WORSHIP

See Top 25 Sights for
US HOLOCAUST MEMORIAL MUSEUM
   (►33)
SHRINE OF THE IMMACULATE CONCEPTION
   (►47)

Washington Jewish Week

Washington Catholics have the National Shrine of the Immaculate Conception; Episcopalians have the National Cathedral. Jewish citizens look to the *Washington Jewish Week*, available at most newsstands, to keep abreast of area events and local Jewish life.

Minaret of the Islamic Mosque and Cultural Center

ADAS ISRAEL CONGREGATION
Conservative congregation.
✉ 2850 Quebec Street NW ☎ 202/362 4433 🚇 Cleveland Park

BET MISH PACHAH SYNAGOGUE
Gay and Lesbian congregation.
✉ Box 141 ☎ 202/833 1638 ❓ Services held at National City Christian Church ✉ 5 Thomas Circle NW

FRANCISCAN MONASTERY AND GARDENS
Byzantine-style monastery with shrines of the Holy Land, underground reproductions of Roman catacombs and the Bishop's Garden specialising in roses.
➕ Off map at L1 ✉ 14th and Quincy Streets NE ☎ 202/526 6800
🕐 Daily 9–5 🚇 Brookland – Catholic University

ISLAMIC MOSQUE AND CULTURAL CENTER
Exclaiming its purpose, the 162-foot minaret calls the faithful five times daily into this centre for all American Moslems. Inside, Arabic art includes Persian carpets, ebony and ivory carvings, stained glass and mosaics.
➕ E2 ✉ 2551 Massachusetts Avenue NW ☎ 202/332 8343
🕐 Cultural Center daily 10:30–4:30, for prayer dawn–10:30PM
🚇 Dupont Circle

KESHER ISRAEL CONGREGATION
Orthodox congregation.
✉ 2801 N Street NW ☎ 202/333 4808 🚇 Foggy Bottom

METROPOLITAN AFRICAN METHODIST EPISCOPAL CHURCH
This red-brick Gothic revival church, known as the national cathedral of the AME movement, was completed in 1886, paid for by ex-slaves and built by African American craftsmen and artisans.
➕ G3 ✉ 1518 M Street NW ☎ 202/331 1426 🕐 Mon–Sat 10–6 🍴 Home-cooked lunch Thu, Fri 11–2 🚇 Farragut North

MOUNT ZION HERITAGE CENTER AND METHODIST CHURCH
This congregation broke from a nearby white group in 1816, educated black children and adults, created the first black library in the District in a nearby building, which they still operate, purchased land for and operated a cemetery for African Americans, and served as a stop on the Underground Railway for

escaped slaves. The late 19th-century brick church is known for its elaborate pressed tin ceiling, wood engravings by African artisans and embellished, cast-iron pillars.

✚ E3 ✉ 1334 29th Street NW ☎ 202/234 0148 🕐 Easily arranged by appointment

ST JOHN'S EPISCOPAL CHURCH

Built by Benjamin Latrobe in a Greek Cross form, the church has later additions including the Doric portico and cupola tower. Pew 54 is reserved for the president, each of whom has worshipped here since the church opened in 1816.

✚ F4 ✉ 1525 H Street NW ☎ 202/347 8766 🕐 Mon–Sat 8–4 🚇 McPherson Square

ST MARY'S EPISCOPAL CHURCH

James Renwick designed this red-brick 1887 Gothic-Revival church for the first black Protestant Episcopal congregation in Washington. The building includes a timber roof and French painted-glass windows depicting St Cyprian and other African religious leaders, and a tiny garden offering quiet in the midst of the downtown bustle.

✚ E4 ✉ 728 23rd Street NW ☎ 202/333 3985 🕐 Daily 9–3 🚇 Foggy Bottom

ST MATTHEW'S CATHEDRAL

President John F Kennedy's funeral mass was held in this plain Renaissance-style church, the seat of Washington's Catholic archbishop. The embellished interior includes stunning mosaics and gilded Corinthian capitals.

✚ F3 ✉ 1725 Rhode Island Avenue ☎ 202/347 3215 🕐 Sun–Fri 7–7, Sat 8–7 🚇 Farragut North

WASHINGTON HEBREW CONGREGATION

Reformed congregation.

✉ 3935 Macomb Street NW ☎ 202/362 7100

WASHINGTON NATIONAL CATHEDRAL

On 30 September 1990 President George Bush and thousands of other guests watched the placement of the final stone of this inspiring Gothic-style building, resplendent with flying buttresses, 565-foot nave, a rose window of 10,500 pieces of stained glass, stone barrel vaults and fanciful gargoyles. The stone-carving in this, the sixth-largest cathedral in the world, is extraordinary: bring binoculars to capture the details and to enhance the view from the Pilgrim Gallery.

✚ C1 ✉ Wisconsin and Massachusetts Avenues NW ☎ 202/537 6200 🕐 May Labor Day: Mon–Fri 10–9, Sat and Sun 10–4:30; Labor Day–30 Apr: daily 10–4:30 🍴 Yes 🚇 Tenley Town; 30 series bus south

Quiet places

Do not overlook the Hall of Remembrance in the US Holocaust Memorial Museum as a place to worship. This space invites quiet, non-denominational contemplation, as does Barnett Newman's *14 Stations of the Cross* hanging on the concourse level of the National Gallery of Art.

Washington National Cathedral

VIEWS

See Top 25 Sights for
CEDAR HILL (►48)
CUSTIS-LEE MANSION AT ARLINGTON
    NATIONAL CEMETERY (►24)
KENNEDY CENTER ROOF TERRACE (►25)
LIBRARY OF CONGRESS CAFETERIA (►46)
US CAPITOL, WEST FACE (►43)
WASHINGTON MONUMENT (►31)

Food with a view

For learning about the city, the clock tower at the Old Post Office has the best view and the building houses a food court with everything from ice cream to Indian food. The tower bells, cast in London in 1976, were donated to Congress to commemorate the American Revolution.

HOTEL WASHINGTON ROOF TERRACE

This national landmark is the oldest continuously operating hotel in the city, known since its opening in 1918 as the hotel with the view. The terrace overlooks the White House and the Washington Monument and is *the* place for afternoon tea or sunset cocktails.

➕ G4 ✉ 515 15th Street NW ☎ 202/638 5900 🕐 14 Apr–30 Oct 11–1 🚇 McPherson Square 💲 Expensive

OLD POST OFFICE BUILDING TOWER

The fanciful, granite 'old tooth' clock tower stands out amid the neo-classical surroundings of the Federal Triangle. The elevator ride to the top allows a close-up view of the city's topography and architecture.

➕ G5 ✉ Pennsylvania Avenue at 12th Street NW ☎ 202/606 8691 🕐 Easter– Labor Day: daily 8AM–11PM; Sep–Mar: daily 10–6 🍴 Yes 🚇 Federal Triangle 💲 Free

The view from the Old Post Office tower

WASHINGTON
where to...

ITALIAN

Prices

Average three-course meal per head, excluding tax and tips

$$$ = over $35

$$ = $20–$35

$ = up to $20

All restaurants mentioned here take the major credit cards. It is usually advisable to make a telephone reservation.

Door-to-door dining

If you find yourself hungry in your room, but don't want room service food, there are several pizza delivery services. Domino's is the largest chain, with many locations. Pizza Hut has a few delivery outlets. Armand's (202/547 6600 on Capitol Hill or 202/363 5500 for upper Wisconsin Avenue), Geppetto (202/333 4315, in Georgetown) and Trio Pizza (202/232 5611, near Dupont Circle) all deliver good pizzas.

GALILEO ($$$)

Known for its wine list, home-made items from breadsticks to mozzarella, and its Italian specialities of grilled fish, game birds and veal, Galileo changes its menu twice daily.

➕ F4 ✉ 1110 21st Street NW ☎ 202/293 7191 🕐 Open for lunch and dinner weekdays, dinner only weekends Ⓜ Foggy Bottom

I MATTI ($$)

The less-expensive sister restaurant to Galileo, i Matti has an extensive menu ranging from pizza to homey polenta, with lots of daily dinner specials such as rabbit cutlet.

➕ F2 ✉ 2436 18th Street NW ☎ 202/462 8844 🕐 Open for lunch and dinner Mon–Sat, dinner only Sun Ⓜ Woodley Park–Zoo

I RICCHI ($$$)

This airy Tuscan dining room, decorated with terracotta tiles and floral frescos, attracts the business crowd with spit-roasted meats and a seasonal menu.

➕ F3 ✉ 1220 19th Street NW ☎ 202/835 0459 🕐 Closed Sat lunch and Sun Ⓜ Dupont Circle

IL RADICCHIO ($)

A young, funky crowd comes here for the all-you-can-eat spaghetti dinner, with a choice of 20 different toppings, and the neighbourhood's café scene.

➕ F3 ✉ 1509 17th Street NW ☎ 202/986 2627 🕐 Closed Sun lunch Ⓜ Dupont Circle

NOTTE LUNA ($$)

This black-and-neon restaurant, near the White House, offers cracker-thin pizzas and innovative pasta specials.

➕ G4 ✉ 809 15th Street NW ☎ 202/408 9500 🕐 Open for lunch and dinner weekdays, dinner only weekends Ⓜ McPherson Square

OTELLO ($)

This quaint restaurant offers inexpensive and simply prepared meat and fish dishes, like red snapper with capers and olives.

➕ F3 ✉ 1329 Connecticut Avenue NW ☎ 202/429 0209 🕐 Open for lunch and dinner Mon–Fri, dinner only Sat, closed Sun Ⓜ Dupont Circle

PIZZERIA PARADISO ($)

This pizzeria, with its trompe l'oeil ceiling, has fresh versions of the basics: pizzas, salads and sandwiches.

➕ F3 ✉ 2029 P Street NW ☎ 202/223 1245 🕐 Open daily for lunch and dinner Ⓜ Dupont Circle

SFUZZI ($–$$)

Popular for happy-hour, with frozen drinks and tasty appetizers, Sfuzzi also has a bistro offering lighter, inexpensive fare such as salads and sandwiches.

➕ J4 ✉ Union Station, 50 Massachusetts Avenue NE ☎ 202/842 4141 🕐 Open daily for lunch and dinner Ⓜ Union Station

TRATTORIA AL SOLE ($$)

The accent is on seafood in this airy restaurant, part of which is in a glass-roofed courtyard.

➕ F3 ✉ 1606 20th Street NW ☎ 202/667 0047 🕐 Closed Sat lunch and Sun Ⓜ Dupont Circle

FRENCH

BISTRO FRANCAIS ($$)

This French country restaurant offers good-value fixed-price lunches and early and late-night dinner specials and stays open until 3AM Sun–Thu, 4AM Fri and Sat.

D3   915 3128 M Street NW   202/338 3830   Open for lunch and dinner daily

GERARD'S PLACE ($$$)

Gerard Pangaud, one of the Washington area's Michelin two-star chefs, merges haute cuisine with New American fare: try the seared tuna.

G4   915 15th Street NW   202/737 4445   Closed Sat lunch and Sun   McPherson Square

JEAN-LOUIS AT THE WATERGATE HOTEL ($$$)

Named for its chef, Jean-Louis Palladin, this restaurant offers contemporary French fare based on the finest regional American ingredients: Louisiana crayfish, wild Oregon mushrooms. Very expensive, but often mentioned as one of the country's best restaurants. The Palladin, upstairs, is less expensive and less formal (202/298 4455).

E4   2650 Virginia Avenue NW (downstairs in the Watergate Hotel)   202/298 4488   No lunches served. Open Tue–Sat. Closed Aug   Foggy Bottom

LA BRASSERIE ($$)

A spot for 'power-breakfasts', the mostly French menu changes daily at this Capitol Hill townhouse restaurant. The crème brulée is reliably excellent.

J5   239 Massachusetts Avenue NE   202/546 9154   Open for breakfast, lunch and dinner daily   Union Station

LA CHAUMIERE ($$)

With the rustic charm of a French country inn, this restaurant serves French provincial fare like pot au feu and bouillabaisse.

E3   2813 M Street NW   202/338 1784   Closed Sat lunch and Sun

LA COLLINE ($$)

Seafood – fricasée, grilled or gratinée – is one measure of this consistently excellent yet reasonably priced Capitol Hill favourite.

J5   400 N Capitol Street NW   202/737 0400   Open for breakfast weekdays; closed Sat lunch and Sun   Union Station

LA FOURCHETTE ($$)

This bit of Paris in Adams-Morgan, with tin ceiling, bentwood chairs and quasi-Post-Impressionist murals offers sturdy bistro cuisine such as veal and lamb shanks.

F2   2429 18th Street NW   202/332 3077   Closed weekend lunch   Woodley Park–Zoo (6 blocks)

LE LION D'OR ($$$)

Some say this was Washington's first national-class restaurant, where you'll find classic French cuisine in an old continental-style room, complete with leather banquettes and tableside service trolleys.

F3   1150 Connecticut Avenue NW (entrance on 18th Street NW)   202/296 7972   Closed Sat lunch and Sun   Farragut North

Quality dining

Long considered a city of mediocre restaurants, Washington in the last few years has come a long way in proving itself to be a city of quality dining. The city has the good fortune to have two chefs who were given two-star ratings by the highly regarded *Guide Michelin*: Jean-Louis Palladin, of Jean-Louis at the Watergate, and Gerard Pangaud, of Gerard's Place.

STEAK & SEAFOOD

Seafood southwest

Washington is filled with restaurants of every imaginable ethnic variety. What it does not have is very many truly good seafood restaurants. But if you have a taste for fish you will find many of the city's seafood restaurants along the southwest waterfront. Head down to Water Street and, in addition to Phillips Flagship, you will find Le Rivage (for French fish dishes), Hogates, Pier Seven, the Gangplank and, for a Cajun twist, Creole Orleans.

GEORGETOWN SEAFOOD GRILL ($$)

This unpretentious Georgetown restaurant brings crabcakes, lobster and softshell crabs to diners in wooden booths. At night, it features a raw bar.

✚ D3 ✉ 3063 M Street NW ☎ 202/333 7038 🕐 Daily lunch and dinner

LES HALLES ($$)

The beef here is American but the preparation is strictly French. There is an upstairs area for cigar smoking.

✚ G5 ✉ 1201 Pennsylvania Avenue NW ☎ 202/347 6848 🕐 Open daily for lunch and dinner Ⓜ Federal Triangle

MORTON'S OF CHICAGO ($$$)

It's not the vinyl-boothed dining room that draws people here, it's the quantity as well as the quality of their steaks. If you're really hungry (or sharing), try the 3-pound porterhouse.

✚ D3 ✉ 3251 Prospect Street NW ☎ 202/342 6258 🕐 Open for dinner only

THE PALM ($$$)

Its plain décor is patterned after the New York original, and the business-like air is matched by the clientele. In addition to huge steaks, the Palm also offers a bargain lunch menu that includes shrimp, veal and chicken salad.

✚ F3 ✉ 1225 19th Street NW ☎ 202/293 9091 🕐 Closed weekend lunch Ⓜ Dupont Circle

PESCE ($$)

Here you can dine on daily seafood specials like roasted monkfish, or buy fresh fish from their fish market.

✚ F3 ✉ 2016 P Street NW ☎ 202/466 FISH 🕐 Mon–Sat lunch and dinner; Sun dinner only Ⓜ Dupont Circle

PHILLIPS FLAGSHIP ($$$)

People come to this enormous seafood restaurant overlooking a marina for large portions, not innovation; the immense seafood buffet is popular with tourists.

✚ G6 ✉ 900 Water Street SW ☎ 202/488 8515 🕐 Open daily for lunch and dinner Ⓜ 6 blocks SW of L'Enfant Plaza Metro stop

PRIME RIB ($$$)

Decorated in black and gold like a 1940s supper club, Prime Rib serves its namesake for the posh meat-and-potatoes set.

✚ F4 ✉ 2020 K Street NW ☎ 202/466 8811 🕐 Closed Sat lunch, Sun Ⓜ Farragut West

SAM AND HARRY'S ($$$)

Understated and genteel, this dining room packs them in with porterhouse and strip steaks, prime rib and daily seafood specials; it also hosts the Evening Star jazz bar.

✚ F3 ✉ 1200 19th Street NW ☎ 202/296 4333 🕐 Closed Sat lunch and Sun Ⓜ Dupont Circle

SEA CATCH ($$$)

This formal Georgetown establishment, hidden in a courtyard overlooking the C & O Canal, has an outstanding raw bar and well-prepared favourites like boiled lobster.

✚ D3 ✉ 1054 31st Street NW ☎ 202/337 8855 🕐 Closed Sun

NEW AMERICAN

CALIFORNIA PIZZA KITCHEN ($)

Bright, shiny and mirrored, this busy restaurant does pizza and pasta the California way.
✚ F3 ✉ 1260 Connecticut Avenue NW ☎ 202/331 4020 🕐 Open daily for lunch and dinner 🚇 Dupont Circle

CITIES ($$)

The front dining area and bar look like a service station. In the back dining room, every few months a different world capital is chosen as the theme, with décor and menu to match.
✚ F2 ✉ 2424 18th Street NW ☎ 202/328 7194 🕐 Closed weekday lunch

KINKEAD'S ($–$$)

You can watch your meal being prepared in the open kitchen upstairs, which specialises in seafood offerings. The bar and café downstairs offer American-style tapas and other inexpensive fare.
✚ F4 ✉ 2000 Pennsylvania Avenue NW ☎ 202/296 7700 Upstairs closed Sun dinner 🚇 Foggy Bottom

NEW HEIGHTS ($$)

Attractively decorated to appeal to discreet celebrities, the frequently changed menu always has vegetarian options like Thai ravioli, and expertly prepared grilled salmon.
✚ E1 ✉ 2317 Calvert Street NW ☎ 202/234 4110 🕐 Closed lunch Mon–Sat 🚇 Woodley Park Zoo

NORA ($$)

The menu changes daily in this attractive exposed-brick and quilt-decorated restaurant. Organic vegetables and free-range meats feature in unusual combinations on the menu, followed by an extensive dessert list.
✚ E3 ✉ 2132 Florida Avenue NW ☎ 202/462 5143 🕐 Closed lunch and Sun 🚇 Dupont Circle

OCCIDENTAL GRILL ($$)

The photo-covered walls may suggest an old Washington club, but while the patrons are loyal, the menu is less conservative, with grilled meats and marinated tuna.
✚ G4 ✉ 1475 Pennsylvania Avenue NW ☎ 202/783 1475 🕐 Open daily for lunch and dinner 🚇 Metro Center

TABARD INN ($$)

With its parlour-like dining rooms and its lovely outdoor dining terrace, the Tabard serves its own organically grown vegetables (in season) and hormone-free beef.
✚ F3 ✉ 1739 N Street NW ☎ 202/833 2668 🕐 Open daily for breakfast, lunch and dinner 🚇 Dupont Circle

1789 ($$$)

Housed in a Federal townhouse with a large fireplace, 1789 specialises in game and seafood.
✚ C3 ✉ 1226 36th Street NW ☎ 202/965 1789 🕐 Open daily for dinner only

701 RESTAURANT ($$)

This very elegant restaurant with large windows looking out on Pennsylvania Avenue, offers tapas, a caviare bar and live jazz every night.
✚ H5 ✉ 701 Pennsylvania Avenue NW ☎ 202/393 0701 🕐 Closed weekend lunch

Hotel restaurants

Some of Washington's best restaurants are in the finer hotels. Among these are Citronelle (New American cuisine, in the Latham Hotel, ➤ 85), the Jefferson Hotel restaurant (New American cuisine), the Morrison-Clark Inn (New American cuisine, ➤ 85) and the John Hay Room (New American cuisine, at the Hay-Adams Hotel, ➤ 84). While they tend toward the expensive, the food and service are generally first-rate.

AMERICAN

Budget meals

If you're on a tight budget, there are many places where you can get a soup, a sandwich and salad for lunch. Many of these better-than-fastfood places are concentrated in the downtown business area bounded by Pennsylvania Avenue, M Street, 14th Street and 21st Street. These places serve mostly office workers and are usually open only on weekdays for breakfast and lunch. Try Au Bon Pain (1615 L Street NW, 1401 I Street NW, 1850 M Street NW or 706 L'Enfant Plaza SW) or the Lunch Box (1719 M Street NW, 1090 Vermont Avenue NW, 1622 I Street NW or 1712 L Street).

AMERICA ($$)

Right in the middle of the hubbub of Union Station, America is an oasis with a something-for-everyone multi-region menu. Southwest specialities are its strong suit.
✚ J4 ✉ Union Station, 50 Massachusetts Avenue NE ☎ 202/682 9555 ⏰ Open daily for lunch and dinner 🚇 Union Station

AMERICAN CAFÉ ($)

This member of a restaurant chain, with its mirrored walls and sleek, modern look, offers a little bit of everything at easily affordable prices.
✚ G4 ✉ The Shops at National Place, 1331 Pennsylvania Avenue NW ☎ 202/626 0770 ⏰ Open daily for lunch and dinner 🚇 Metro Center

GEORGIA BROWN'S ($$)

This elegant New Southern restaurant, with its conversation nooks, is beloved by government officials, lobbyists, and journalists. Pork, lima beans and okra turn into haute cuisine here.
✚ G4 ✉ 950 15th Street NW ☎ 202/393 4499 ⏰ Closed Sat lunch 🚇 McPherson Square

HARD ROCK CAFÉ ($)

This international chain celebrates rock music with memorabilia and loud music. The rather ordinary menu is best for hamburgers and cherry pie.
✚ G4 ✉ 999 E Street NW ☎ 202/737 ROCK ⏰ Open daily for lunch and dinner 🚇 Metro Center

THE MONOCLE ($$$)

With fireplaces and the many photos of politicians adorning the walls, this is one of the best restaurants for spotting members of Congress at lunch and dinner. The food is American with a Continental touch.
✚ J5 ✉ 107 D Street NE ☎ 202/546 4488 ⏰ Closed Sat lunch and Sun 🚇 Union Station

OLD EBBITT GRILL ($$)

One block from the White House, this is one of Washington's busiest restaurants, with oyster bar, pub food and family fare.
✚ G4 ✉ 675 15th Street NW ☎ 202/347 4800 ⏰ Open daily for breakfast, lunch and dinner 🚇 Metro Center

OLD GLORY ($$)

The flags of six big barbecue-eating Southern states hang from the ceiling in this popular (and usually crowded) updated roadhouse diner, which serves all variations of barbecued pork, beef and chicken.
✚ D3 ✉ 3139 M Street NW ☎ 202/337 3406 ⏰ Open daily for lunch and dinner

PLANET HOLLYWOOD ($)

Owned by movie stars Bruce Willis, Demi Moore, Sylvester Stallone and Arnold Schwarzenegger, this famous chain is to movies what Hard Rock is to music. The menu includes beef, turkey and vegetarian burgers, and desserts such as Arnie's mother's apple strudel.
✚ G5 ✉ 1101 Pennsylvania Avenue NW ☎ 202/783 STAR ⏰ Open daily for lunch and dinner 🚇 Federal Triangle

INDIAN, AFRICAN & MIDDLE EASTERN

ADITI ($)

This elegant, two-level Indian restaurant, with burgundy carpets and chairs and pale mint-coloured walls with brass sconces, is known for its consistently high quality breads and curries. The second floor overlooks Georgetown's busy M Street.

D3 ⊠ 3299 M Street NW ☎ 202/625 6825 ⓞ Open daily for lunch and dinner

BACCHUS ($$)

An intimate Lebanese restaurant in an English basement; you can easily put together a meal from their long list of appetisers.

F3 ⊠ 1827 Jefferson Place NW ☎ 202/785 0734 ⓞ Closed Sat lunch and Sun ⓠ Dupont Circle

THE BOMBAY CLUB ($$)

Located just a block from the White House, this beautiful Indian restaurant, with its potted palms and a bright blue ceiling over white plaster mouldings, tries to recapture the feel of a private club for British colonials in 19th-century India. The breads are first-rate, and seafood dishes such as lobster Malabar help justify the expense.

F4 ⊠ 815 Connecticut Avenue NW ☎ 202/659 3727 ⓞ Open for dinner daily, lunch Mon–Fri, brunch Sun ⓠ Farragut West

BUKOM CAFÉ ($)

Sunny African pop music, a palm-frond-and-kente-cloth décor and a spicy West African menu with goat, lamb, chicken and vegetable entrées brighten this narrow two-storey dining room. There is live music nightly, and they serve food until late.

F2 ⊠ 2442 18th Street NW ☎ 202/265 4600 ⓞ Open for dinner Tue–Sun, lunch Sat. Closed Mon ⓠ 6 blocks from Woodley Park–Zoo

MARRAKESH ($$)

Located on a block of auto repair and supply shops, this Moroccan restaurant features a fixed-price feast shared by everyone at your table and eaten without cutlery. Belly dancers put on a nightly show.

H4 ⊠ 617 New York Avenue NW ☎ 202/393 9393 ⓞ Closed lunch ⓠ Gallery Place – Chinatown

SKEWERS ($)

As the name suggests, the speciality of this Middle Eastern restaurant is kebabs – meat, vegetable or shrimp – served with almond-flaked rice or pasta. If the restaurant is too crowded, try the cheap California eats downstairs at Café Luna (☎ 202/387 4005) or the reading room/coffee house upstairs at Luna Books (☎ 202/332 2543).

F3 ⊠ 1633 P Street NW ☎ 202/387 7400 ⓞ Open daily for lunch and dinner ⓠ Dupont Circle

ZED'S ETHIOPIAN CUISINE ($)

One of many Ethiopian restaurants in the city, this Georgetown outpost stakes its claim not with its simple décor but with its tangy *njera*, a bubbly bread used to dip into spicy meat and vegetable stews.

D3 ⊠ 3318 M Street NW ☎ 202/333 4710 ⓞ Open daily for lunch and dinner.

Adams-Morgan eating

Adams-Morgan, the most ethnically diverse part of town, is a crowded, bustling and interesting neighbourhood, filled with a variety of restaurants. A walk along 18th Street will take you past Saigonnais (Vietnamese, 2307 18th Street), Argentine Grill (Argentine, 2433 18th Street), Meskerem (Ethiopian, 2434 18th Street), Montego Café (Jamaican, 2437 18th Street), the Star of Siam (Vietnamese, 2446 18th Street), Fasika's (Ethiopian, 2447 18th Street) and Straits of Malaya (Indonesian, 1836 18th Street).

ORIENTAL

Chinatown

Washington's idea of Chinatown is a several block area around 7th and H Streets NW. The area is somewhat run down but there are some good restaurants. Of course, everyone has his or her own favourites but among some of the better ones are Hunan Chinatown (624 H Street NW), Mr Yung's (740 6th Street NW), China Inn (631 H Street NW), Tony Cheng's Mongolian Restaurant (619 H Street NW) and Full Kee (509 H Street NW). A few other ethnic restaurants have entered the area, including Burma (740 6th Street NW upstairs), serving Burmese food, of course.

BENKAY ($$)
You can order from the menu, but the main attraction here is the buffet of sushi, tempura and other Japanese foods, available at lunch and dinner.
🔛 G4 ✉ 727 15th Street NW, lower level ☎ 202/737 1515 🕐 Closed weekend lunch 🚇 McPherson Square

BUSARA ($$)
A Thai restaurant, stylish in black rubber, brushed steel and lacquered tables, that stands out of the crowd with unusual items such as red curry duck and cellophone noodles with three kinds of mushroom.
🔛 C2 ✉ 2340 Wisconsin Avenue NW ☎ 202/337 2340 🕐 Open daily for lunch and dinner

CAFE ASIA ($)
The décor is spartan and the staff few, but low prices and the choice of cuisines – Singaporean, Indonesian, Japanese, Thai, Chinese and Vietnamese – makes queuing worth while.
🔛 F3 ✉ 1134 19th Street NW ☎ 202/659 2696 🕐 Closed Sun 🚇 Dupont Circle

LITTLE VIET GARDEN ($)
This and the nearby Queen Bee (3181 Wilson Boulevard, ☎ 703/527 3444) are among the many Vietnamese restaurants to be found in Arlington, VA. The Little Viet Garden has terrace dining in season.
🔛 A5 ✉ 3012 Wilson Boulevard, Arlington, VA ☎ 703/522 9686 🕐 Open daily for lunch and dinner

SAIGON GOURMET ($$)
Service is brisk and friendly at this popular, French-influenced Vietnamese dining room; try the grilled pork with rice crêpes.
🔛 E1 ✉ 2635 Connecticut Avenue NW ☎ 202/265 1360 🕐 Open daily for lunch and dinner 🚇 Woodley Park–Zoo

SALA THAI ($$)
Mirrored walls and soft lights soften the ambience of this small downstairs Thai restaurant, where noodles and curries are favourites.
🔛 F3 ✉ 2016 P Street NW ☎ 202/872 1144 🕐 Open daily for lunch and dinner 🚇 Dupont Circle

SARINAH SATAY HOUSE ($)
This delightful Indonesian restaurant resembles an indoor garden, with real trees growing through the ceiling. Satays, combination plates and crisp *loempia* all feature on the menu.
🔛 D3 ✉ 1338 Wisconsin Avenue NW ☎ 202/337 2955 🕐 Closed Sun lunch and Mon

STAR OF SIAM ($$)
This Thai restaurant's dishes, including squid salad, are among the most reliable in the city.
🔛 F3 ✉ 1136 19th Street NW ☎ 202/785 2839 🕐 Closed Sun lunch 🚇 Dupont Circle

UNKAI ($$$)
In contrast to its modern grey and black décor, this restaurant offers *kaiseki*, an aristocratic style of Japanese cuisine rarely available to the public.
🔛 E3 ✉ 1250 24th Street NW ☎ 202/466 2299 🕐 Closed Sat lunch, Sun 🚇 Dupont Circle

TEX-MEX, SPANISH & LATIN

AUSTIN GRILL ($)
Hot adobe pastels and Texas music set the scene at this popular spot, which draws a young crowd for sizzling *fajitas* (chicken or steak) and chips with salsa.
✚ C2 ✉ 2404 Wisconsin Avenue NW ☎ 202/337 8080 🕐 Open daily for lunch and dinner

COCO LOCO ($$$)
This is two restaurants in one; a tapas bar and a Brazilian *churrasqueria* – grilled meat brought to your table and sliced on to your plate. Wed–Sat nights, half of the restaurant is an up-market night club.
✚ H4 ✉ 810 7th Street NW ☎ 202/289 2626 🕐 Closed weekend lunch 🚇 Gallery Place–Chinatown

THE GRILL FROM IPANEMA ($$)
This focuses on Brazilian cuisine, from spicy seafood stews to grilled steak and other hearty meat dishes. Try traditional *feijoada*, a stew of black beans, pork and smoked meat, served Wed and Sat.
✚ F2 ✉ 1858 Columbia Road NW ☎ 202/986 0757 🕐 Closed lunch Mon–Fri 🚇 Woodley Park–Zoo

JALEO ($$)
Although entrées are available, the long list of hot and cold tapas is the house speciality.
✚ H5 ✉ 480 7th Street NW ☎ 202/628 7949 🕐 Open daily for lunch and dinner 🚇 Archives–Navy Memorial

LAS PAMPAS ($$)
Grilled fresh fish and some Tex-Mex staples supplement the traditional, mostly beef, Argentine menu. Upstairs, a South-western *cantina* comes alive weekend nights.
✚ D3 ✉ 3291 M Street NW ☎ 202/333 5151 🕐 Open daily for lunch and dinner

LAURIOL PLAZA ($$)
The specialities of this simply decorated Spanish/ South American restaurant includes gazpacho, *ceviche* and tongue.
✚ F2 ✉ 1801 18th Street NW ☎ 202/387 0035 🕐 Open daily for lunch and dinner 🚇 Dupont Circle

PEYOTE CAFÉ ($)
Located below Roxanne Restaurant (from whose Southwestern menu you may order), this pub has standard Tex-Mex items as well as vegetarian dishes.
✚ F2 ✉ 2319 18th Street NW ☎ 202/462 8330 🕐 Closed weekday lunch 🚇 7 blocks from Woodley Park–Zoo

RED SAGE($$$)
The over-the-top Southwestern décor includes a pseudo-adobe warren of dining rooms. Peppers in everything but desserts, and portions and prices are big. There is a chilli bar and café upstairs.
✚ G4 ✉ 605 14th Street NW ☎ 202/638 4444 🕐 Closed Sun lunch 🚇 Metro Center

TABERNA DEL ALABARDERO ($$$)
The formal dining room, high-class service, plush Old World décor and handsome bar create a romantic atmosphere in which to nibble classic Spanish tapas or savour seafood paella.
✚ F4 ✉ 1776 I Street NW (entrance on 18th Street) ☎ 202/ 429 2200 🕐 Closed Sat lunch and Sun 🚇 Farragut West

Bethesda feasting

Bethesda, just across the District line in Maryland, has in the past few years become a veritable city of restaurants. There are at least two dining guides available, each listing about 175 establishments and including information on hours, attire and parking. The *Bethesda Dining Guide* is free and is available from the Bethesda Urban Partnership (7908 Woodmont Avenue, Bethesda ☎ 301/215 6660). Another, moderately priced, guide, *The World's Most Complete Guide to Bethesda's Restaurants*, is available at bookstores such as Borders, Olsson's, Waldenbooks and B Dalton and at some CVS Pharmacies.

SHOPPING DISTRICTS, MALLS & DEPARTMENT STORES

Multi-purpose malls

US shopping malls are a cultural phenomenon, serving as walking tracks for senior citizens in the early morning, recreation centres for latch-key pre-teens after school, and town centres for young mothers on rainy days. Each has a subtle individual character, even when the shops are multi-national chains.

ADAMS-MORGAN

Within three blocks of 18th Street NW and Columbia Road, Bohemian, eccentric, multi-cultural Adams-Morgan offers a bewildering range of experiences for the dedicated shopper. Antique shops special-ising in the 1950s, Afro-centric apparel and accessories, a Haitian art gallery, a kosher grocery, jewellery hand-crafted by local artisans, and Skynear and Company (✉ 1800 Wyoming Avenue NW ☎ 202/797 7160), the most unusual home decorating shop in the city, are all to be found here.

CITY PLACE MALL

City Place Mall offers discounted brand-name merchandise at Nordstrom Rack, Ross, Marshall, Shoe Rack, 9 West and four dozen other retailers; 10 cinemas and a food court.
✚ Off map to north ✉ 8661 Colesville Road, Silver Spring MD ☎ 301/589 1091 ◷ Mon–Sat 10–9, Sun 12–6 Ⓜ Silver Spring

CONNECTICUT AVENUE

Connecticut Avenue above Dupont Circle provides a lively mix of restaurants and shops offering modern furniture, housewares, shoes and gourmet coffee shops which support the book stores lining the avenue. Connecticut below the circle is home to up-market department stores and boutiques, especially for women.

EASTERN MARKET

Gentrified Capitol Hill retains the Eastern Market, home on Saturday to a lively produce market and on Sunday to an open-air antique and import bazaar. Surrounding the market are antique stores and second-hand clothing shops, one specialising in men's apparel. Here, too, the croissant and coffee culture has invaded so you can get fresh roasted beans, brioche and grilled vegetable sandwiches. For breakfast or lunch, don't overlook the Market Lunch, which provides old-style ham and eggs, enormous flap-jacks with rich blueberry topping, and the city's best crab cakes.
✚ K6 ✉ Pennsylvania Avenue & 7th Street SE Ⓜ Eastern Market

FASHION CENTER

Macy's and Nordstrom anchor the 160 shops at Fashion Center at Pentagon City. Nordstrom's practices are credited with reviving retail service in America. The clerks here know the stock intimately and are superbly trained to assist the customer whether you are browsing, replacing a ripped stocking or buying a fur coat. If you have hard-to-fit feet, try Nordstrom's, which originally began life as a shoe store.
✚ D8 ✉ 1100 Hayes Street at Army-Navy Drive and I-395 ☎ 703/415 2400 ◷ Mon–Sat 10–9:30; Sun 11–6 Ⓜ Pentagon City

GEORGETOWN PARK

The spacious, posh three-level Georgetown Park is a delight for anyone heading through the lively streets to Wisconsin and M, the heart of Georgetown shopping. Many galleries, antiques stores and boutiques are within easy walking distance. The crowd jostling you on this corner is young, hip and on its way up. There is a wide range of apparel and decorator shops for the tasteful and well-to-do.

� D3 ✉ 3222 M Street NW ☎ 202/298 5577 ⏰ Mon–Sat 10–9; Sun noon–6

HECHT AND COMPANY

Affectionately known as 'Hecht's', this well-laid-out department store will satisfy diverse tastes, from conservative to trendy. There is also a walk-in Ticketmaster sales counter for area shows, concerts and sports events at rock-bottom prices.

� G4 ✉ 12th & G Streets NW ☎ 202/628 6661 ⏰ Mon–Sat 9–8; Sun noon–6 🚇 Metro Center

MAZZA GALLERIE

Mazza Gallerie has the ritzy Neiman Marcus department store and a discount Filene's Basement, along with 40 other shops offering gourmet cookware (Williams-Sonoma, Laura Ashley Home), up-market women's shoes (Stephane Kelian); maternity wear for the very fashion conscious (Pea in the Pod); and one-of-a-kind furnishings and gifts with something of a Southwestern flavour (Skynear and Company).

� Off map to north ✉ 5300 Wisconsin Avenue NW ☎ 202/686 9515 ⏰ Mon–Fri 10–8; Sat 10–6; Sun noon–5 🚇 Friendship Heights

POTOMAC MILLS MALL

This is the local daddy of discount shopping and has now become the largest tourist attraction in Virginia, 30 miles south of DC off I-95.

� Off map to south ✉ 3900 Potomac Mills Circle, Prince William, VA ☎ 703/643 1770 ⏰ Mon–Sat 10–9:30; Sun 11– 6 🚌 Shuttle from DC ☎ 703/878 1262

WOODWARD AND LOTHROP

This huge department store offers no fewer than eight floors of shopping, and is particularly good for clothing – women's, men's and children's. Gourmet foods and home furnishings also feature strongly. You could do worse than to revive yourself in the tearoom afterwards.

� G4 ✉ 11th & F Streets NW ☎ 202/347 5300 ⏰ Mon–Sat 9–8; Sun noon–6 🚇 Metro Center

Stay cool

Washington summers are only bearable because of air conditioning, and the malls crank up the coolers to accommodate shoppers, diners and movie-goers. And there is always a sale. In the words of the 'shop till you drop' crowd, 'If you paid full price, you're not playing the game right.'

BOOKS & MUSIC

Books for nightowls

You can find book shops open well into the night in nearly every area of Washington, many with cafés, knowledgeable staff and discounts. There is always a place to browse after a day's sightseeing or business meetings.

BOOKWORKS: WASHINGTON PROJECT FOR THE ARTS

Bookworks specialises in artists' books and small presses.

➕ G5 ✉ 400 7th Street NW ☎ 202/347 4590 🕐 Tue–Sat 11–6 Ⓜ Archives–Navy Memorial

BORDERS BOOKS AND MUSIC

Borders is a national chain, offering 325,000 titles (including 50,000 music titles), and leading the book sellers' industry by combining book and music sales, a café, daily readings, book signings, and literary and musical events. Helpful, knowledgeable staff encourage browsing, listening and reading in this spacious, well-lit store.

➕ F3 ✉ 18th and L Streets, NW ☎ 202/466 4999 🕐 Mon–Fri 8AM–10PM; Sat 9–9; Sun 11–7 Ⓜ Farragut West

CHAPTERS LITERARY BOOKSTORE

Specialising in poetry, fiction and literary criticism, Chapters takes books seriously: no cartoon books, just real books for readers.

➕ F3 ✉ 1512 K Street NW ☎ 202/347 5495 🕐 Mon–Fri 10–6:30; Sat 11–5 Ⓜ McPherson Square

CROWN BOOKS

This national chain specialises in best-sellers, crafts, popular psychology, fiction and the 'kiss'n'tell' books so loved by Washington scandal-mongers. Everything is heavily discounted,

especially the overloaded remainders table that can be found at the front of every store.

➕ F3 ✉ 11 Dupont Circle NW ☎ 202/319 1374 🕐 Daily 9AM–midnight Ⓜ Dupont Circle; ➕ F4 ✉ 2020 K Street NW ☎ 202/659 2030 🕐 Mon–Fri 9–7, Sat and Sun 10–6

KEMP MILL MUSIC

This local chain keeps prices low on a full range of CDs and tapes. All branches are open Mon–Thu 10–10; Fri–Sat 10–midnight; Sun 11–7.

➕ D3 ✉ 1254 Wisconsin Avenue NW ☎ 202/333 1392; ➕ F3 ✉ 1518 Connecticut Avenue NW ☎ 202/332 8247 Ⓜ Farragut North; ➕ F2 ✉ 2459 18th Street NW ☎ 202/387 1011 Ⓜ Dupont Circle; ➕ F4 ✉ 1900 L Street NW ☎ 202/223 5310 Ⓜ Farragut West; ➕ C1 ✉ 4000 Wisconsin Avenue NW ☎ 202/364 9704

KRAMERBOOKS & AFTERWORDS CAFÉ

This is the quintessential Washington literary pick-up scene.

➕ F4 ✉ 1517 Connecticut Avenue NW ☎ 202/387 1400 🕐 Weekends 24 hours; Mon–Thu 7:30AM–1AM Ⓜ Dupont Circle

LAMBDA RISING BOOK STORE

An intriguingly named store which offers gay and lesbian books and gifts.

➕ E3 ✉ 1625 Connecticut Avenue NW ☎ 202/462 6969 🕐 Daily 9–12 Ⓜ Dupont Circle

LAMMAS BOOKSTORE

A great selection of books by and for women.

➕ E3 ✉ 1426 21st Street NW ☎ 202/775 8218 🕐 Mon–Sat 10–9; Sun 11–7 Ⓜ Dupont Circle

MELODY RECORD SHOP

Knowledgeable staff and a 10 per cent – 40 per cent discount on CDs, cassettes and tapes are particular attractions here.

🞣 F3 ✉ 1623 Connecticut Avenue NW ☎ 202/232 4002 🕔 Mon–Thu 10–11; Fri–Sat 10–midnight; Sun noon–10 Ⓜ Farragut North

OLSSON'S BOOKS & RECORDS

A comprehensive stock covering most areas of publishing, plus recordings which specialise in classical and folk music in many formats.

🞣 D3 ✉ 1239 Wisconsin Avenue, NW ☎ 202/338 9544 🕔 Mon–Thu 10AM–11PM; Fri–Sat 10AM–midnight; Sun 12–7

ORPHEUS RECORDS

This shop stocks all styles of music in every format, but vinyl hunters are attracted by high-quality used LPs and the best selection of new vinyl in the city especially rock'n'roll, jazz and blues.

🞣 D3 ✉ 3249 M Street NW ☎ 202/337 7970 🕔 Mon–Sat 11–11; Sun noon–8

POLITICS AND PROSE

This is the largest independent book store in the area. You will find comfortable reading chairs, an inviting coffee shop and knowledgeable staff.

🞣 Off map at E1 ✉ 5015 Connecticut Avenue NW ☎ 202/364 1919 🕔 Sun–Thu 8:30AM–10PM; Fri–Sat 8:30–midnight Ⓜ VanNess, then 15 minutes walk north

SECOND STORY BOOKS

If used books are your passion, start here. If you don't find what you are looking for on the acres of shelves, maybe your treasure is hiding at Second Story's warehouse. They also offer a very helpful nationwide search service for out-of-print books.

🞣 F3 ✉ 2000 P Street NW ☎ 202/659 8884 🕔 Daily 10–10 Ⓜ Dupont Circle

SERENADE RECORD SHOP

A store which is strong on classical but carries almost everything else in all formats, except LPs.

🞣 F3 ✉ 1800 M Street NW ☎ 202/452 0075 🕔 Mon–Sat 10–8; Sun 11–6

SISTER'S SPACE & BOOKS

A specialist store for books by and about African American women.

🞣 G2 ✉ 1354 U Street NW ☎ 202/332 3433 🕔 Tue–Fri 10–7; Sat 10–6; Sun noon–5 Ⓜ U Street–Cardozo

TOWER RECORDS

Loud and hip, here is the largest selection of cassettes and CDs in Washington. The selection covers jazz, rock, soul and classical.

🞣 E4 ✉ 2000 Pennsylvania Avenue NW ☎ 202/331 2400 🕔 Daily 9am–midnight Ⓜ Foggy Bottom

US GOVERNMENT BOOKSTORE

Here are the countless publications produced by the Feds, including research reports on American history, home improvements, internal revenue studies, energy, environmental improvements, health and nutrition.

🞣 G4 ✉ 1510 H Street NW ☎ 202/653 5075 🕔 Mon–Fri 9–4:30 Ⓜ McPherson Square

Special-interest tomes

Speciality books can be located in the hundreds of professional associations, think tanks, and foundations that make Washington home – the Bookings Institute, the Carnegie Endowment for International Peace, the Freedom Forum, the American Association of Museum, the American Institute of Architects, even the American Society of Association Executives. If you've got an interest in architecture, bee-keeping, chemistry, or zoology you can find both popular and scholarly editions to inform and challenge every aspect of your passion.

VINTAGE SECOND-HAND SHOPPING & MUSEUM SHOPS

Tax-exempt shopping

Even tiny museums and historic houses carefully create retail space. Cedar Hill, for instance, offers a wide selection of books on African American history. Because these are non-profit tax-exempt organisations, the customer is not charged sales tax at museum shops, making a saving of 7 per cent on all purchases.

MUSEUM SHOPS

The gift shops of Washington museums offer some of the best shopping anywhere, and no serious shopper should overlook them. The Smithsonian is the area's third-largest retailer.

In addition to book stores geared to a museum's topic – modern art, African culture, American politics and history, architecture or whatever – museum shops offer reproduction furnishings and decorative arts, jewellery and apparel relating to the museum's collection. The Hirshhorn Museum offers modern jewellery; the National Museum of American History has reproduction 19th-century toys, kitchenware and handmade quilts; the Corcoran Museum offers blown-glass objects and woven scarves; the Building Museum sells tools and architectural puzzles.

Alphabets and cartoon animation can be bought from a tiny area at the front desk of the National Children's Museum. The Department of Interior acts as an outlet for Native American art and crafts. Bonsai pots and pruning gear can be found at the National Arboretum; herbs from the Bishop's Garden at Washington National Cathedral. Hillwood offers Russian icons, porcelain, cloisonné and Native American dream-catchers and pottery. The latest stamps can be purchased and posted at the National Postal Museum. Kids love the dried ice creams at the National Air and Space Museum and the dinosaurs at the National Museum of Natural History. T-shirts, an American export, can be found everywhere to fit every taste and body form.

ONCE IS NOT ENOUGH

Come here for used but stylish men's, women's and children's clothing and accessories at terrific prices.

✚ A2 ✉ 4830 MacArthur Boulevard NW ☎ 202/337 3072 🕐 Mon–Sat 10–5

THE OPPORTUNITY SHOP OF THE CHRIST CHILD SOCIETY

Operated for charitable purposes, this shop sells vintage clothing, quality housewares and consigned antiques.

✚ D3 ✉ 1427 Wisconsin Avenue NW ☎ 202/333 6635 🕐 Mon–Sat 10–3:45

SECONDI

This second-floor consignment shop in the heart of Dupont Circle features fashions from Gap to Chanel for both men and women.

✚ F3 ✉ 1611 Connecticut Avenue NW ☎ 202/667 1122 🕐 Mon–Sat 11–6, Thu 11–7 🚇 Dupont Circle

UNIFORM

Uniform traps you in time: feathered mules with lucite heels, knee-high full skirts, three-button suits, clutch bags, lava lamps and chunky plastic jewellery.

✚ F2 ✉ 2318 18th Street NW ☎ 202/483 4577 🕐 Mon noon–7; Wed–Fri noon–8; Sat 11–8; Sun noon–6 🚇 Dupont Circle

ANTIQUES, CRAFTS & COLLECTABLES

THE AMERICAN HAND

This gallery-shop sells one-of-a-kind and limited edition ceramics, textiles and wood crafts.

✚ E3 ✉ 2906 M Street NW ☎ 202/965 3273 🕐 Mon–Sat 11–6; Sun 1–5

APPALACHIAN SPRING

Seek this out for ceramics, quilts, fine wood work and other traditional and contemporary crafts.

✚ D3 ✉ 1415 Wisconsin Avenue NW ☎ 202/337 5780

CHENONCEAU ANTIQUES

Here are American 19th- and 20th-century antiques chosen by someone with a sophisticated knowledge of this period.

✚ F2 ✉ 2314 18th Street NW ☎ 202/667 1651 🕐 Thu–Sun

CHERISHABLES

Cherishables emphasises 18th-century Federal furniture and decorations.

✚ F3 ✉ 1608 20th Street NW ☎ 202/785 4087 🕐 Mon–Sat 11–6

GEORGETOWN ANTIQUES CENTER

Victorian art nouveau and art deco objects are displayed in an accommodating Victorian town house.

✚ E3 ✉ 2918 M Street NW ☎ 202/338 3811 🕐 Mon–Sat 11–6; Sun noon–5

G K S BUSH

Browse among early American high-style furniture and related art.

✚ E3 ✉ 2828 Pennsylvania Avenue NW ☎ 202/965 0653 🕐 Mon–Fri 10–6; Sat 10–5

INDIAN CRAFT SHOP

Two outlets showcase hand-crafted Eskimo walrus-ivory carving, Zuni pots, Hopi dolls and Navajo pottery.

✚ D3 ✉ Georgetown Park, 3222 M Street NW ☎ 202/342 3918 🕐 Mon–Sat 10–9; Sun noon–6; ✚ F5 ✉ Department of Interior, 1849 C Street NW, Room 1023 ☎ 202/208 4056 🕐 Mon–Fri 8:30–4:30 🚇 McPherson Square

MARSTON LUCE

This gallery is chock full of American folk art, weathervanes and geometric textiles.

✚ F5 ✉ 314 21st Street NW ☎ 202/775 9460 🕐 Mon–Sat 11–6

THE PHOENIX

The place to come for Mexican folk crafts, silver jewellery, and natural-fibre native and contemporary clothing.

✚ D3 ✉ 1514 Wisconsin Avenue NW ☎ 202/338 4404 🕐 Mon–Fri 10–6, Sat–Sun 11–5

RETROSPECTIVE

Retrospective sells the things baby-boomers grew up on in the 1940s and 1950s: streamlined designs in metal furniture, clunky tableware and bold patterns.

✚ F2 ✉ 2324 18th Street NW ☎ 202/483 8112 🕐 Mon–Fri noon–7; Sat 11–7; Sun noon–6. Closed Tue

SUSQUEHANNA

Susquehanna specialises in American furniture and works of art in the largest antique space in Georgetown.

✚ D3 ✉ 3216 O Street NW ☎ 202/333 1511 🕐 Mon–Sat

Treasure-hunting

Georgetown, Adams-Morgan, Dupont Circle and the 7th Street art corridor are abundantly supplied with galleries, boutiques and speciality shops. An afternoon shopping excursion will no doubt yield trinkets and treasures for the entire family.

CLOTHING

Understated elegance

Washingtonians cultivate a studied dowdiness of dress. High-fashion shopping is limited to the Watergate and Willard hotels, but if you want office or tourist attire, you can get great buys almost everywhere.

BRITCHES OF GEORGETOWN

Stylish men come to the two branches of this store for trendy but traditional clothing in natural fibres.

🔲 F3 ✉ 1219 Connecticut Avenue NW ☎ 202/347 8994 🕐 Mon–Wed, Fri, Sat 10–6, Thu 10–8 🚇 Dupont Circle; 🔲 D3 ✉ 1247 Wisconsin Avenue NW ☎ 202/338 3330 🕐 Mon–Wed, Fri, Sat 10–6, Thu 10–8

BROOKS BROTHERS

An American institution, Brooks has been outfitting American men since 1818, which makes it the oldest men's speciality store in the nation.

🔲 F4 ✉ 1840 L Street NW ☎ 202/659 4650 🕐 Mon–Wed, Fri, Sat 9:30–6, Thu 9:30–7 🚇 Farragut West

BURBERRYS

The store which introduced Americans to the trench coat; the British company also manufactures traditional, high-quality men's and women's apparel.

🔲 F3 ✉ 1155 Connecticut Avenue NW ☎ 202/463 3000 🕐 Mon–Wed, Fri, Sat 9:30–6, Thu 9:30–7, Sun noon–5 🚇 Dupont Circle

CHANEL

Chanel has its largest store in America, full of pricey, desirable women's clothes and accessories, at the Willard Hotel.

🔲 G4 ✉ 1455 Pennsylvania Avenue, NW ☎ 202/638 5055 🕐 Mon–Fri 10–5 🚇 Metro Center

FORECAST

Forecast's experienced buyer works hard for the individualistic females who frequent this shop.

🔲 K6 ✉ 218 7th Street SE ☎ 202/547 7337 🕐 Tue–Sat 10–5 🚇 Eastern Market

HUGO BOSS

Classic fabrics and silhouettes from this well-known German designer.

🔲 F3 ✉ 1201 Connecticut Avenue NW ☎ 202/887 5081 🕐 Mon–Wed, Fri, Sat 10–6:30, Thu 10–7 🚇 Farragut North

J PRESS

J Press provides the Ivy League look, as it has since 1902 when it was founded at Yale University.

🔲 F4 ✉ 1801 L Street NW ☎ 202/857 0120 🕐 Mon–Sat 9:30–6 🚇 Farragut West

KHISMET WEARABLE ART

A combination of original designs with African fabrics creates unusual and beautiful garments for women's day and evening wear.

🔲 F2 ✉ 1800 Belmont Road NW ☎ 202/234 7778 🕐 Wed–Sat 1–8; Sun 1–6 🚇 Dupont Circle

KOBOS

Kobos imports West African clothing, accessories and African music.

🔲 F2 ✉ 2444 18th Street NW ☎ 202/332 9580 🕐 Mon–Sat 11–7, Sun 12–6 🚇 Dupont Circle

RIZIK BROTHERS

Designer clothing combines with expert service in this famous Washington ladies' outfitters.

🔲 F3 ✉ 1100 Connecticut Avenue NW ☎ 202/223 4050 🕐 Mon–Sat 9–6; Thu until 8 🚇 Farragut North

GOURMET FOODS & SPECIALITY STORES

DEAN & DELUCA

Occupying one of the 19th-century farmers' markets on Georgetown's main street, this New York gourmet store offers thousands of quality products, from bakery goods and double-fat cheese to rich red meats, to designer vegetables, prepared salads and elegant entrées for one or many.

🔲 D3 ✉ 3276 M Street NW
☎ 202/342 2500 🕐 Sun–Thu
10–8; Fri, Sat 10–9

EASTERN MARKET

Eastern Market, unrestored and retaining its neighbourhood character, sells the freshest produce to be had in the city, particularly during harvest seasons, when farmers from Maryland and Virginia come to market on Saturday morning. On Sunday the tin-roofed arcade shelters a lively flea market.

🔲 K6 ✉ 7th and C Streets SE
☎ 202/546 2698 🕐 Tue–Sat
7–6, Sun 9–4 🚇 Eastern Market

THE FRENCH MARKET

This market has been educating the American palate for 50 years to home-made pâtés, escargots, baguettes, croissants and French cheeses.

🔲 D2 ✉ 1626-32 Wisconsin
Avenue NW ☎ 202/338 4828
🕐 Tue–Sat 8:30–6

FRESH FIELDS

This small national chain succeeded in a saturated market because of absolute top quality, mostly organic, fresh foods

with old-fashioned customer service. The oatmeal cookies with maple sugar icing can't be bettered anywhere, at any price!

🔲 Off map to north-west
✉ 1649 Rockville Pike
☎ 301/984 4880 Mon–Sat
8–9; Sun 8–8 🚇 Twin Brook

A LITTERI

At this location since 1932, this Italian speciality shop is in the heart of the capital city's wholesale food market, worth the short cab ride necessary from downtown DC. Litteri's features more than 40 brands of imported olive oil and wines to go with every pasta dish known to mankind.

🔲 K3 ✉ 517 Morse Street NE
☎ 202/544 0183 🕐 Tue–
Wed 8–4; Thur–Fri 8–5; Sat 8–3

LAWSON'S

Lawson's caters to a single professional population with home-made salads, prepared entrées, salad bar, wine selections and full bakery.

🔲 F3 ✉ 1350 Connecticut
Avenue NW ☎ 202/775 0400
Mon–Fri 7:30–8; Sat 10–6
🚇 Dupont Circle

RED SAGE GENERAL STORE

An outgrowth of the popular Southwestern restaurant next door, this store sells chillies and hot-hot-hot to mild salsa, fancy olive oils and herbal vinegars, fresh-baked breads and desserts.

🔲 G4 ✉ 14th and F streets NW
☎ 202/638 3276 🕐 Mon–Thu
8–7, Fri 8–9, Sat 8–8 🚇 Metro
Center

The speciality boom

Speciality food stores have arrived, in essence replacing local produce markets, which once supplied the populace. A recent phenomenon, the up-market coffee shop, satisfies the coffee cult which seems to have invaded the city in the past few years. You can get your tall, double, de-caf cup with a twist on almost any corner.

THEATRES

Tickets

Tickets to most events are available at the box office or through one of three main ticket outlets. TicketMaster (☎ 202/432 7328) sells tickets by phone or at selected stores to concerts, sports events and many special events. Protix (☎ 703/218 6500) has tickets to shows at Wolf Trap and some other venues. TicketPlace (☎ 202/842 5387) sells half-price, day-of-performance tickets for selected shows (it is also a full-price TicketMaster outlet); tickets must be bought in person at Lisner Auditorium (✉ 730 21st Street NW ⊕ Tue–Fri noon–4, Sat 11–5; tickets for Sun and Mon performances sold on Sat. Only cash is accepted; there is a 10 per cent service charge per order.

ARENA STAGE

Arena manages a long season in its three theatres: the theatre-in-the-round Arena, the proscenium Kreeger and the cabaret-style Old Vat Room. The New Voices series offers reduced prices to see developing shows.

✚ H7　✉ 6th Street and Maine Avenue SW　☎ 202/488 3300　⊕ Waterfront

FORD'S THEATRE

Now mostly presenting musicals (Dickens's *A Christmas Carol* is presented at Christmas every year), this is the theatre where President Abraham Lincoln was assassinated.

✚ G4　✉ 511 10th Street NW　☎ 202/347 4833　⊕ Metro Center

GALA HISPANIC THEATRE

This company presents Spanish classics as well as contemporary and modern Latin American plays in both Spanish and English.

✚ F1　✉ 1625 Park Road NW　☎ 202/234 7174

KENNEDY CENTER

Kennedy Center is Washington's busiest cultural centre, hosting a wide variety of events, including ballet, modern dance, drama and experimental theatre.

✚ E4　✉ New Hampshire Avenue and Rock Creek Parkway　☎ 202/467 4600 or 800/444 1324　⊕ Foggy Bottom

NATIONAL THEATRE

Destroyed by fire and rebuilt four times, the National Theatre has operated in the same location since 1835. It presents pre- and post-Broadway shows.

✚ G4　✉ 1321 Pennsylvania Avenue NW　☎ 202/628 6161　⊕ Metro Center

SHAKESPEARE THEATRE

The Shakespeare's season includes four plays, three by the Bard and one by one of his contemporaries.

✚ H5　✉ 450 7th Street NW　☎ 202/393 2700　⊕ Archives–Navy Memorial

SOURCE THEATRE

The 107-seat Source Theatre presents established plays and modern interpretations of classics. Each July and August, Source hosts a series of new plays, many by local playwrights.

✚ G2　✉ 1835 14th Street NW　☎ 202/462 1073　⊕ U Street–Cardozo

STUDIO THEATRE

One of Washington's nicest independent company theatres, Studio performs a mix of classics and offbeat plays. The 50-seat Secondstage presents experimental works.

✚ G3　✉ 1333 P Street NW　☎ 202/332 3300　⊕ Dupont Circle

WARNER THEATRE

After a two-year major restoration, the Warner reopened in 1992 and now hosts theatre and dance performances, as well as some pop music shows.

✚ G4　✉ 13th and E Streets NW　☎ 202/783 4000　⊕ Metro Center

CONCERT HALLS

DAR CONSTITUTION HALL

Formerly home to the National Symphony Orchestra, this 3,700-seat hall hosts musical performances, staged shows and the occasional big-name comedy act.
F5 ✉ 18th and D Streets NW ☎ 202/638 2661 ⓜ Farragut West (6 blocks north)

GEORGE MASON UNIVERSITY

The GMU campus in suburban Virginia is home to the Center for the Arts. The Patriot Center, also on campus, holds concerts and sporting events.
Off map to south ✉ Route 123 and Braddock Road, Fairfax, VA ☎ Center for the Arts, 703/993 8888; Patriot Center, 703/993 3000 or 202/432 7328

LISNER AUDITORIUM

This 1,500-seat theatre, located on the campus of George Washington University, presents pop, classical and choral music performances.
F4 ✉ 21st and H Streets NW ☎ 202/994 6800 ⓜ Foggy Bottom

MERRIWEATHER POST PAVILION

Located one hour north of Washington, this outdoor pavilion with some covered seating hosts big-name pop acts during the summer months.
Off map to north ✉ Columbia, MD ☎ 301/982 1800 or 301/596 0660

NATIONAL GALLERY OF ART

The National Gallery Orchestra, as well as outside recitalists and ensembles, hold free concerts in the West Building's West Garden Court on Sunday evenings from October to June.
H5 ✉ 6th Street and Constitution Avenue NW ☎ 202/842 6941 or 202/842 6698 ⓜ Archives–Navy Memorial

NISSAN PAVILION AT STONE RIDGE

This 25,000-seat venue opened in 1995 near Manassas, VA, about one hour from Washington.
Off map to south ✉ 7800 Cellar Door Drive, Gainesville, VA ☎ 703/549 7625 or 202/432 7328

SMITHSONIAN INSTITUTION

A wide assortment of music – both free and ticketed – is presented by the Smithsonian at various indoor and out-door locations. The Smithsonian Associates Program (☎ 202/357 3030) offers everything from a cappella groups to Cajun zydeco bands, as well as other kinds of events.
G5, H5, H4 ✉ At various Smithsonian museums, most of which are on the Mall ☎ 202/357 2700 ⓜ Smithsonian

USAIR ARENA

This 18,000-seat arena, home to the Washington Capitals hockey and Washington Bullets basketball teams, is also one of the area's top venues for big-name pop, rock, and rap acts.
Off map to east ✉ 1 Harry S Truman Drive, Landover, MD ☎ 301/350 3400 or 202/432 7328

Kennedy Center

Kennedy Center is indeed a centre for cultural events, with five separate stages under one roof: the Concert Hall, home to the National Symphony Orchestra; the Opera House, the stage for ballet, modern dance, grand opera and large-scale musicals; the Eisenhower Theater, usually used for drama; the Terrace Theater, a smaller stage for chamber groups and experimental works; and the Theater Lab.

BARS & LOUNGES

Where the action is

Washington has many pockets of activity, mostly centred around the downtown business district or more ethnically diverse neighbourhoods. Adams-Morgan, around 18th Street and Columbia Road, has many bars, clubs and restaurants. Capitol Hill (especially along Pennsylvania Avenue SE), the U Street NW corridor (from about 14th Street to 18th Street) and the downtown area around 19th and M Streets NW are also fairly dense with similar night activities.

Listings

The Washington Post is the leading daily. The Friday 'Weekend' section lists entertainment and special events. The Sunday edition carries a guide to the 'lively arts'. The *City Paper*, delivered on Thursdays, is a free alternative weekly with the best calendar of current events. The monthly *Washingtonian Magazine* reviews restaurants and performances and provides in-depth coverage of the city.

BRICKSKELLER
With more than 500 brands of beer for sale, from Central American lagers to US microbrewed ales, this is Washington's premier pub. Bartenders oblige beer-can collectors by opening the containers from the bottom. ✚ E3 ✉ 1523 22nd Street NW ☎ 202/293 1885 🕐 Open Mon–Thu 11:30AM–2AM, Fri 11:30AM–3AM, Sat 6PM–3AM, Sun 6PM–2AM 🚇 Dupont Circle

CAPITOL CITY BREWING COMPANY
This microbrewery, the first brewery in Washington since Prohibition, features a gleaming copper bar, with metal steps leading up to where the brews are actually made. Capitol City makes everything from a bitter to a bock, though not all types are available at all times. ✚ G4 ✉ 1100 New York Avenue NW ☎ 202/628 2222 🕐 Open Mon–Sat 11AM–2AM, Sun 11AM–midnight 🚇 Metro Center

CHAMPIONS
One of DC's biggest sports bars, the walls are covered with jerseys, pucks, bats and balls, and the evening's big game is always on the big screen. ✚ D3 ✉ 1206 Wisconsin Avenue NW ☎ 202/965 4005 🕐 Open Mon–Thu 5PM–2AM, Fri 5PM–3AM, Sat 11:30AM–3AM, Sun 11:30AM–2AM. One-drink minimum Fri and Sat after 10PM.

THE DUBLINER
The closest thing in Washington to an Irish pub, this is a favourite with Capitol Hill staffers. ✚ J4 ✉ 520 North Capitol Road NW ☎ 202/737 3773 🕐 Open Sun–Thu 11AM–1:30AM, Fri–Sat 11AM–2:30AM 🚇 Union Station

15 MINS
This club has a bit of everything in its several rooms: live music, movies on a large-screen TV, a couple of pool tables and a DJ playing recorded music. A favourite spot for the mostly college-age set. Cover charge. ✚ G4 ✉ 1030 15th Street NW ☎ 202/408 1855 🕐 Open Mon–Tue 5PM–2AM, Wed–Thu noon–2AM, Fri noon–3AM, Sat 8PM–3AM 🚇 McPherson Square

HAWK'N'DOVE
A friendly neighbourhood bar, frequented mostly by political types, lobbyists and Marines (from a nearby barracks). ✚ J6 ✉ 329 Pennsylvania Avenue SE ☎ 202/543 3300 🕐 Open Sun–Thu 10AM–2AM, Fri and Sat 10AM–3AM 🚇 Capitol South

SIGN OF THE WHALE
This well-known post-Preppie/neo-Yuppie haven is right in the heart of a densely bar-populated area of downtown. ✚ F3 ✉ 1825 M Street NW ☎ 202/785 1110 🕐 Open Sun–Thu 11:30AM–2AM, Fri and Sat 11:30AM–3AM 🚇 Farragut North

YACHT CLUB
Just across the border into Maryland, this lounge is popular with well-dressed, middle-aged singles. Jacket and tie required (casual Wed.) ✚ Off map to north-west ✉ 8111 Woodmont Avenue, Bethesda, MD ☎ 301/654 2396 🕐 Open Tue–Thu 5PM–1AM, Fri 5PM–2AM, Sat 8PM–2AM.

NIGHT CLUBS (LIVE MUSIC)

THE BAYOU

This long-time Georgetown rock club showcases national acts and local talent. Every variety of rock music is covered. Tickets are available at the door or through TicketMaster. Occasional no-alcohol, all-ages shows allow those under 18 a chance to dance. Cover charge. No credit cards.

✚ D4 ✉ 3135 K Street NW ☎ 202/333 2897 ⏰ Generally open daily 8PM–2AM

BIRCHMERE

The best place in the area to hear nationally known acoustic folk and bluegrass acts, with the occasional rockabilly or rock act.

✚ Off map ✉ 3901 Mount Vernon Avenue, Alexandria, VA ☎ 703/549 5919 ⏰ Open Sun–Thu 6:30PM–11PM, Fri–Sat 7PM–12:30AM

BLUES ALLEY

Washington's best jazz club, it serves up national jazz acts, such as Ramsey Lewis and Charlie Byrd, as well as Creole cooking. Cover charge and minimum charge.

✚ D3 ✉ Rear 1073 Wisconsin Avenue NW ☎ 202/337 4141 ⏰ Open Sun–Thu 6PM–midnight, Fri and Sat 6PM–2AM. Shows at 8 and 10, plus occasional midnight shows Fri and Sat

CAFÉ LAUTREC

They play jazz every night in this club with Toulouse-Lautrec décor and French food. Come on Friday or Saturday and watch tap dancer Johne Forges dance on the tabletops. Minimum charge Tue and Thu–Sun.

✚ F2 ✉ 2431 18th Street NW ☎ 202/265 6436 ⏰ Open Sun–Thu 5PM–2AM, Fri and Sat 5PM–3AM

9:30 CLUB

This trendy club is dark, hot in the summer, cold in the winter and always smoky, but it has possibly the best array of local, national, and international progressive music. Cover charge. Get tickets at the door or from TicketMaster.

✚ G4 ✉ 930 F Street NW ☎ 202/393 0930 ⏰ Generally open Sun–Thu 7:30PM–midnight, Fri–Sat 9PM–2AM ⓜ Metro Center

ONE STEP DOWN

Like a good jazz club should be, One Step Down is smoky, low-ceilinged and intimate, with the best jazz jukebox in town. It books many local acts, and often features New York jazz artists. Live music is presented Thu–Mon. Cover charge and minimum charge.

✚ E4 ✉ 2517 Pennsylvania Avenue NW ☎ 202/331 8863 ⏰ Open Mon–Thu 10AM–2AM, Fri 10AM–3AM, Sat noon–3AM, Sun noon–2AM ⓜ Foggy Bottom

TORNADO ALLEY

Although outside the city, it's worth the short drive here to see some of the best American 'roots music', such as blues, Cajun, zydeco, and anything else that comes into musical public forefront. Cover charge.

✚ Off map to north ✉ 11319 Elkin Street, Wheaton, MD ☎ 301/929 0795 ⏰ Generally open Tue–Thu 5PM–1AM, Fri and Sat 5PM–2AM, Sun 5PM–1AM

Night options

The night clubs of Washington, scattered throughout the city, offer every kind of music. You can have it live or played by a DJ. There can be dancing or just listening. Another popular activity is the murder mystery dinner, a whodunit where the audience gets involved with the story while watching it. The Blair Mansion Inn (✉ 7711 Eastern Avenue, Silver Spring, MD ☎ 301/588 1689) and the Murder Mystery Dinner Theatre (✉ Old Europe, 2434 Wisconsin Avenue NW ☎ 202/333 6875) have weekend shows.

MISCELLANEOUS ARTS

Films

Check the daily newspapers for mainstream first-run films; cinemas are scattered throughout the city. For revivals and foreign, independent and avant-garde films, try the American Film Institute (✉ Kennedy Center ☎ 202/785 4600), the Biograph (✉ 2819 M Street NW ☎ 202/333 2696) or the Key (✉ 1222 Wisconsin Avenue NW ☎ 202/333 5100). The Hirshhorn Museum (☎ 202/357 2700), National Gallery of Art East Building (☎ 202/737 4215), and National Archives (☎ 202/501 5000), all on the Mall, often show historical, unusual, or experimental films. Filmfest DC (☎ 202/274 6810), an annual citywide festival of international cinema, takes place in late April and early May.

American folklife

The Smithsonian's Festival of American Folklife provides an alternative to high culture and fine art. Each year the Smithsonian celebrates one country, one state, one profession and a number of musical folk traditions. Summer temperatures persuade bureaucrats and others to join in the early evening, open-air dance parties enjoyed by all ages.

CHAMBER MUSIC

Corcoran Gallery of Art ✉ 17th Street and New York Avenue NW ☎ 202/638 3211 🕐 One Friday each month, Oct–May, plus some summer dates

Folger Shakespeare Library The Folger Consort plays medieval, Renaissance and baroque music ✉ 201 East Capitol Street SE ☎ 202/544 7077 🕐 Oct–May

National Academy of Sciences Free performances from October to May ✉ 2101 Constitution Avenue NW ☎ 202/334 2436 🕐 Oct–May 🎫 Free

Phillips Collection ✉ 1600 21st Street NW ☎ 202/387 2151 🕐 Sep–May, Sun at 5PM

CHORAL GROUPS

Choral Arts Society A 180-voice choir performs at the Kennedy Center (➤ 25) ☎ 202/244 3669 🕐 Sep–Apr, plus three Xmas sing-alongs in Dec

Washington National Cathedral Choral and church groups frequently perform in the cathedral (➤ 59) ☎ 202/537 6200

National Shrine of the Immaculate Conception Venue for choral groups (➤ 47) ☎ 202/526 8300

COMEDY CLUBS

Dropping the Cow Improvisational comedy at Square One Theatre ✉ Wisconsin Avenue and Q Street NW ☎ 202/829 0529 🕐 Sat

The Comedy Café Wednesday is open-mike night, Thursday is local talent, and on Friday and Saturday, well-known comedians perform ✉ 1520 K Street NW ☎ 202/638 5653

The Improv Well-known comedians perform ✉ 1140 Connecticut Avenue NW ☎ 202/296 7008

CONCERT SERIES

Armed Forces Concert Series On the East Terrace of the Capitol and at the Sylvan Theater in the Washington Monument grounds ☎ 202/767 5658 (Air Force); ☎ 703/696 3718 (Army); ☎ 202/433 2525 (Navy); ☎ 202/433 4011 (Marines) 🕐 Jun–Aug; weekday evenings

Carter Barron Amphitheater Pop, jazz and gospel music. During two weeks in June the Shakespeare Theatre (➤ 78) presents a free play by the Bard in this outdoor venue ✉ 16th Street and Colorado Avenue NW ☎ 202/426 6837 🕐 Mid-Jun–Aug, Sat and Sun evenings

Washington Performing Arts Society Books performers in halls around the city ☎ 202/833 9800

DANCE

Dance Place Modern and ethnic dance ✉ 3225 8th Street NE ☎ 202/269 1600 🕐 most weekends

Joy of Motion The home of several area troupes ✉ 1643 Connecticut Avenue NW ☎ 202/387 0911

Mount Vernon College Hosts visiting dance companies in the autumn and spring ✉ 2100 Foxhall Road NW ☎ 202/625 4655

Smithsonian Associates Program Dance groups performing at various Smithsonian museums ☎ 202/357 3030

The Washington Ballet Various ballet performances, plus *The Nutcracker* in December ☎ 202/362 3606) 🕐 Oct, Feb May and Dec

SPORTS

BIKING

For information on bike trails in and around Washington, contact the Washington Area Bicyclist Association (✉ 1819 H Street NW, Suite 640, 20006 ☎ 202/872 9830, fax 202/862 9762). Some of the best rides are along the George Washington Memorial Parkway, which runs along the Virginia side of the Potomac River all the way to Mount Vernon (35 miles round-trip); on the C & O Canal towpath from Georgetown to Cumberland, MD (180 miles one-way); and through Rock Creek Park).

Rent bikes from:
Bicycle Exchange (near the Mount Vernon Trail) ✉ 1506-C Belle View Boulevard, Alexandria, VA ☎ 703/768 3444
Big Wheel Bikes (near the C & O Canal towpath) ✉ 1034 33rd Street NW, Georgetown ☎ 202/337 0254
City Bikes (near the Rock Creek bike path) ✉ 2501 Champlain Street NW ☎ 202/265 1564
Fletcher's Boat House ✉ C & O Canal towpath, 2 miles north of Georgetown, near Reservoir Road NW ☎ 202/244 0461
Metropolis Bike & Scooter (also rents rollerblades) ✉ 709 8th Street SE, Capitol Hill ☎ 202/ 543 8900
Thompson's Boat Center ✉ Virginia Avenue and Rock Creek Park, behind Kennedy Center ☎ 202/333 4861
Tow Path Cycle ✉ 823 S Washington Street, Alexandria, VA ☎ 703/549 5368

BOATING

Fletcher's Boat House (see Biking, above), rents rowing boats and canoes
Thompson's Boat Center (at Virginia Avenue and Rock Creek Parkway behind the Kennedy Center) rents canoes, rowing boats, rowing shells and sailboards ☎ 202/333 4861
Paddle boats are available during the summer on the east side of the Tidal Basin in front of the Jefferson Memorial ☎ 202/484 0206

GOLF

Washington has three public golf courses:
The Hains Point course ✉ East Potomac Park near the Jefferson Memorial ☎ 202/863 9007
Langston Golf Course ✉ 26th Street and Benning Road NE ☎ 202/397 8638
Rock Creek Park ✉ 16th and Rittenhouse Streets NW ☎ 202/882 7332

Suburban public courses:
Reston National ✉ 11875 Sunrise Valley Drive, Reston, VA ☎ 703/620 9333
Northwest Park ✉ 15701 Layhill Road, Wheaton, MD ☎ 301/598 6100
Enterprise ✉ 2802 Enterprise Road, Mitchellville, MD ☎ 301/249 2040

TENNIS

The District of Columbia has 144 outdoor courts. Permits to use them are issued free by the Department of Recreation; send a self-addressed, stamped envelope for a permit and a list of courts, or call for information ✉ Department of Recreation, 3149 16th Street NW, 20010 ☎ 202/673 7646

Spectator sports

In addition to participant sports activities, Washington also offers spectator sports. If you are here in autumn you will hear about the Redskins, the football team, but season-ticket holders have all the seats. You'll have better luck seeing the Bullets play basketball or the Capitals play hockey, both at the USAir Arena in Landover, MD. For tickets, call TicketMaster ☎ 202/432 7328.

LUXURY HOTELS

Prices

Expect to pay $180 or more for a double room in a luxury hotel (excluding tax, plus $1.50 per night occupancy tax).

Booking agencies

Capitol Reservations books rooms at over 70 better hotels at rates 20–40 per cent lower than normal; call 202/452 1270 or 800/847 4832 weekdays 9–6; they also offers packages with tours and meals. Washington DC Accommodations will book rooms in any hotel in town, with discounts of 20–40 per cent available at about 40 locations; call 202/289 2220 or 800/554 2220 weekdays 9–5.

FOUR SEASONS HOTEL

Located on the eastern edge of Georgetown, this hotel is known as a gathering place for Washington's élite.

☐ E3 ☒ 2800 Pennsylvania Avenue NW ☎ 202/342 0444 or 800/332 3442 (fax 202/342 1673) ⓜ Foggy Bottom

GRAND HYATT

The spectacular lobby looks like a Mediterranean hillside village from a movie set. A dining area surrounds a blue lagoon.

☐ G4 ☒ 1000 H Street NW ☎ 202/582 1234 or 800/233 1234 (fax 202/637 4718) ⓜ Metro Center

HAY-ADAMS HOTEL

Looking like a mansion in disguise, this hotel's south-side rooms offer a picture-postcard view of the White House. Rooms are decorated in English-country-house fashion.

☐ F4 ☒ 1 Lafayette Square NW ☎ 202/638 6600 or 800/424 5054 (fax 202/638 2716) ⓜ McPherson Square

HOTEL WASHINGTON

The Hotel Washington is known for its outdoor rooftop terrace with a view of the White House grounds and the Washington Monument.

☐ G4 ☒ 515 15th Street NW ☎ 202/638 5900 (fax 202/638 1594) ⓜ McPherson Square

PARK HYATT

A notable collection of modern art adorns this hotel. The rooms, a mix of traditional and contemporary styles, are accented with reproductions of Chinese antiques.

☐ E3 ☒ 1201 24th Street NW ☎ 202/789 1234 or 800/233 1234 (fax 202/457 8823) ⓜ Foggy Bottom

THE RITZ-CARLTON

With European furnishings and 18th- and 19th-century English art, the décor is English hunt-club.

☐ F3 ☒ 2100 Massachusetts Avenue NW ☎ 202/293 2100 or 800/241 3333 (fax 202/466 9867) ⓜ Dupont Circle

RITZ-CARLTON, PENTAGON CITY

Just across the Potomac River from DC, this hotel features a $2 million art and antiques collection displayed in its public areas. Many rooms have a view of the monuments across the river.

☐ D8 ☒ 1250 S Hayes Street Arlington, VA ☎ 703/415 5000 or 800/241 3333 (fax 703/415 5060) ⓜ Pentagon City

STOUFFER RENAISSANCE MAYFLOWER

The ornate lobby glistens with gilded trim. The rooms feature custom designed furniture.

☐ F4 ☒ 1127 Connecticut Avenue NW ☎ 202/347 3000 or 800/468 3571 (fax 202/466 9083) ⓜ Farragut North

WATERGATE HOTEL

While best known for its part in the fall of Richard Nixon, this distinctive hotel also houses two restaurants featuring one of the few two-star Michelin chefs in the US.

☐ E4 ☒ 2650 Virginia Avenue NW ☎ 202/965 2300 or 800/424 2736 (fax 202/337 7915) ⓜ Foggy Bottom

MODERATELY PRICED HOTELS

BELLEVUE HOTEL
The public rooms on the main floor are modelled after great halls in old manor houses.
J4 ✉ 15 E Street NW
☎ 202/638 0900 or 800/327 6667 (fax 202/638 5132)
Ⓜ Union Station

CAPITOL HILL SUITES
This all-suite hotel is tucked away behind the Madison Building of the Library of Congress.
J6 ✉ 200 C Street SE
☎ 202/543 6000 or 800/424 9165 (fax 202/547 2608)
Ⓜ Capitol South

GEORGETOWN DUTCH INN
This all-suite hotel, on a side street in Georgetown, has a homely ambience.
D4 ✉ 1075 Thomas Jefferson Street NW ☎ 202/337 0900 (fax 202/333 6526)

GUEST QUARTERS
With two locations, these all-suite hotels are close to Georgetown and the Kennedy Center.
E4 ✉ 801 New Hampshire Avenue NW ☎ 202/785 2000 or 800/424 2900 (fax 202/785 9485) Ⓜ Foggy Bottom; E4 ✉ 2500 Pennsylvania Avenue NW ☎ 202/333 8060 or 800/424 2900 (fax 202/338 3818) Ⓜ Foggy Bottom

HENLEY PARK HOTEL
Offering a bit of Britain in a developing neighbourhood, the Henley Park is one of the National Trust for Historic Preservation's designated Historic Hotels.
G4 ✉ 926 Massachusetts Avenue NW ☎ 202/638 5200 or 800/222 8474 (fax 202/638 6740) Ⓜ Mt Vernon Square–UDC

INN AT FOGGY BOTTOM
This European-style eight-storey hotel is only a few blocks from Georgetown. Half the rooms are suites. Complimentary continental breakfast.
E4 ✉ 824 New Hampshire Avenue NW ☎ 202/337 6620 (fax 202/298 7499) Ⓜ Foggy Bottom

LATHAM HOTEL
This small, colonial-style hotel on one of Georgetown's main streets offers views of busy M Street or the C & O Canal. The popular Citronelle Restaurant is one of Washington's best.
D3 ✉ 3000 M Street NW ☎ 202/726 5000 or 800/ 368 5922 (fax 202/337 4250)

MORRISON-CLARK INN HOTEL
Created by merging two 1864 town houses, this inn is also one of the National Trust for Historic Preservation's designated Historic Hotels. The restaurant is highly rated.
G4 ✉ Massachusetts Avenue and 11th Street NW ☎ 202/898 1200 or 800/332 7898 (fax 202/289 8576) Ⓜ Mt Vernon Square–UDC

RIVER INN
This small, all-suite hotel is steps from Georgetown, George Washington University and the Kennedy Center. The rooms are homely and modest.
E4 ✉ 924 25th Street NW ☎ 202/337 7600 or 800/424 2741 (fax 202/625 2618) Ⓜ Foggy Bottom

Prices
Expect to pay between $100 and $180 for a double room in a mid-range hotel (excluding tax, plus $1.50 per night occupancy tax).

Washington hotels
Most major chains have hotels in the city and the nearby suburbs. For a complete list of hotels, contact the Washington, DC, Convention and Visitors Association (✉ 1212 New York Avenue NW, Washington, DC 20005 ☎ 202/789 7000). All of the hotels here are air-conditioned. Nearly all of the finer hotels have superb restaurants whose traditionally high prices are almost completely justified.

BUDGET ACCOMMODATION

Prices

Expect to pay under $100 for a double room in budget accommodation (excluding tax, plus $1.50 per night occupancy tax).

Bed & breakfast

To find reasonably priced accommodation in small guest houses and private homes, contact either of the following bed-and-breakfast services: Bed 'n' Breakfast Accommodations Ltd of Washington, DC (✉ Box 12011, Washington, DC 20005 ☎ 202/328 3510) or Bed and Breakfast League, Ltd (✉ Box 9490, Washington, DC 20016 9490 ☎ 202/363 7767). If you require a private bathroom, make this clear at time of booking.

DAYS INN CONNECTICUT AVENUE

This standard hotel is away from the busy downtown area but only two blocks from the Metro.

✚ Off ma to north-west ✉ 4400 Connecticut Avenue NW ☎ 202/244 5600 or 800/325 2525 (fax 202/244 6794) Ⓜ Van Ness

HOLIDAY INN CAPITOL HILL

A bargain for the budget-minded traveller; children under age 18 stay free.

✚ J5 ✉ 415 New Jersey Avenue NW ☎ 202/638 1616 or 800/638 1116 (fax 202/347 1813) Ⓜ Judiciary Square

HOTEL TABARD INN

Consisting of three joined Victorian town houses, the Tabard was named after the hostelry of Chaucer's *Canterbury Tales*. Furnishings are charmingly well-worn.

✚ F3 ✉ 1739 N Street NW ☎ 202/785 1277 (fax 202/785 6173) Ⓜ Dupont Circle

HOWARD JOHNSON KENNEDY CENTER

Located close to the Kennedy Center and Georgetown, this American institution offers large and comfortable rooms.

✚ E4 ✉ 2601 Virginia Avenue NW ☎ 202/965 2700 or 800/654 2000 (fax 202/965 2700 ext 7910) Ⓜ Foggy Bottom

HOWARD JOHNSON'S NATIONAL AIRPORT

Located in the nearby suburb of Crystal City, this hotel offers a free shuttle service to the Metro and to National Airport.

✚ E9 ✉ 2650 Jefferson Davis Highway (Route 1), Arlington, VA ☎ 703/684 7200 or 800/278 2243 (fax 703/684 3217) Ⓜ Crystal City

KALORAMA GUEST HOUSE

Five separate turn-of-the-century town houses, decorated with old-fashioned charm. No phones or TV. Complimentary breakfast and afternoon aperitifs.

✚ F2 ✉ 1854 Mintwood Place NW ☎ 202/667 6369 (fax 202/319 1262); ✉ 2700 Cathedral Avenue NW ☎ 202/328 0860 (fax 202/319 1262)

NORMANDY INN

This European-style hotel is on a quiet street in the exclusive embassy area of Connecticut Avenue. There is a wine and cheese reception every Tuesday evening.

✚ E2 ✉ 2118 Wyoming Avenue NW ☎ 202/483 1350 or 800/424 3729 (fax 202/387 8241)

WASHINGTON INTERNATIONAL AYH-HOSTEL

This well-kept hostel has dormitory rooms with 250 bunk beds; families are given their own room if the hostel is not full.

✚ G4 ✉ 1009 11th Street NW ☎ 202/737 2333 (fax 202/737 1508) Ⓜ McPherson Square

WINDSOR PARK HOTEL

Rooms in this small hotel are decorated with Queen Anne-style furnishings and period art. Each room has a small refrigerator. Free continental breakfast.

✚ E2 ✉ 2116 Kalorama Road NW ☎ 202/483 7700 or 800/247 3064 (fax 202/332 4547)

WASHINGTON
travel facts

ARRIVING & DEPARTING

Before you go

- British citizens need a valid 10-year passport to enter the US.
- You don't need a visa unless you plan to stay longer than 90 days, your trip is for other than pleasure, you have ever been refused a visa or refused entry to the US, or if you don't have a return or onward ticket.

When to go

- In spring, the most crowded season, the city is alive with flowers and blossoming trees, including the must-see-to-believe cherry blossoms around the Tidal Basin and Washington Monument.

Climate

- Washington has two lovely seasons: spring and autumn, with average high temperatures of between 15°C and 25°C.
- Summers are very hot and humid, with temperatures sometimes reaching 35°C or more.
- Winters are unpredictable: a year of record cold weather and below-freezing temperatures was recently followed by one of the warmest winters ever.
- Snowfall is equally unpredictable, but when snowstorms do occur, they tend to shut the city down.

Arriving by plane

- Direct international flights to Washington arrive at either Dulles International Airport (☎ 703/661 2700), 26 miles west in Virginia, or Baltimore-Washington International (BWI) Airport (☎ 410/859 7032), 25 miles northeast in Maryland.
- National Airport (☎ 703/419 8000), in Virginia, 4 miles south of downtown Washington, handles domestic flights only. While often cramped and crowded (although an expansion is being undertaken), National has the advantage of being a 20-minute Metro ride from the city centre.
- Taxi to downtown: the fare for one person to downtown from National is about $13 (plus a $1.25 surcharge); from Dulles, $45; and from BWI, $50.

Bus to downtown

- Washington Flyer (☎ 703/685 1400) goes from National and Dulles airports to 1517 K Street, where a free shuttle bus serves several hotels. The trip from National takes 20 minutes and costs $8 ($14 round-trip); from Dulles, the 45-minute ride costs $16 ($26 round-trip). An inter-airport service between Dulles and National is also available for about $16 ($26 round-trip). Fares may be paid with cash, MasterCard or Visa; children under 6 ride free.
- BWI SuperShuttle buses (☎ 800/809 7080) leave BWI hourly for 1517 K Street NW. The 65-minute ride costs $15 ($25 round-trip); drivers accept cash, travellers' cheques and major credit cards.

Train to downtown

- Free shuttle buses run between airline terminals and the train station at BWI airport.
- Amtrak (☎ 800/872 7245) and MARC (Maryland Rail Commuter Service, ☎ 800/325 7245) trains run between BWI and Washington's Union Station from around 6AM to midnight.
- The cost of the 40-minute ride is $10 on Amtrak, $4.50 on MARC (weekdays only).

Limousine to downtown

- Diplomat Limousine (☎ 703/461 6800) will chauffeur you downtown from National or Dulles for about $75, $90 from · BWI. Book at least a day ahead.
- Private Car (☎ 800/685 0888) has a counter at BWI airport ($62 to downtown) or call ahead to have a car waiting for you at National ($45 to downtown) or Dulles ($75).
- Some hotels provide van service to and from the airports; check with your hotel.

Customs regulations

- British visitors aged 21 or over may import duty-free the following into the US: 200 cigarettes or 50 cigars or 2kg of tobacco; one litre of alcohol; gifts valued up to $200.
- Restricted items include meat products, seeds, plants and fruits.

ESSENTIAL FACTS

Travel insurance

- Make sure you have a policy covering accident, medical expenses, personal liability, trip cancellation, delayed departure and loss or theft of personal property.
- Before you leave, make sure you will be covered if you have a pre-existing medical condition or are pregnant; your insurers may not pay for routine or continuing treatment or may require a note from your doctor certifying your fitness to travel.
- The Association of British Insurers (ABI), a trade association representing 450 insurance companies, advises extra medical coverage for visitors to the United States. Contact the ABI at ✉ 51 Gresham Street, London EC2V

7HQ ☎ 0171/600 3333; ✉ 30 Gordon Street, Glasgow G1 3PU ☎ 0141/226 3905; ✉ Scottish Provident Building, Donegall Square W, Belfast BT1 6JE ☎ 01232/249176.

Opening hours

- Stores: Mon–Sat 10–7 (or 8). Some have extended hours on Thursday; those in shopping or tourist areas often open Sun 10/noon–5/6.
- Banks: Mon–Fri 9–3. Some stay open until 5 on Friday, or close at 2 and open again from 4 to 6.
- Museums: daily 10–5.30; some have extended hours on Thursday. Many private museums are closed Monday or Tuesday and some museums in government office buildings are closed weekends. The Smithsonian often sets extended spring and summer hours annually for some of its museums (☎ 202/357 2700 for details).

National holidays

- New Year's Day (1 January)
- Martin Luther King Day (third Monday in January)
- Presidents Day (the third Monday in February)
- Memorial Day (the last Monday in May)
- Independence Day (4 July)
- Labor Day (the first Monday in September)
- Thanksgiving Day (the fourth Thursday in November)
- Christmas Day (25 December)
- Banks, post offices and most government agencies are closed for these holidays, although most museums and stores are open.

Money matters

- The unit of currency is the dollar (= 100 cents). Notes (bills) come in denominations of $1, $5, $10, $20, $50 and $100; coins are 25¢ (a quarter), 10¢ (a dime), 5¢ (a nickel) and 1¢ (a penny, increasingly optional).

- Nearly all banks have Automatic Teller Machines (ATMs), which accept cards registered in other countries that are linked to the Cirrus or Plus networks. Before leaving home, check which network your cards are linked to and ensure your personal identification number is valid in the US, where six-figure numbers are the norm.

- Credit cards are a widely accepted and secure alternative to cash.

- US dollar travellers' cheques function like cash in all but small shops; $20 and $50 denominations are the most useful. Don't bother trying to exchange these (or foreign currency) at the bank – it is more trouble than it's worth and commissions are high.

- Money and travellers' cheques can be exchanged at many banks and at a few hotels, or at Thomas Cook Currency Services (✉ 1800 K Street NW ☎ 202/872 1233 and Union Station, 50 Massachusetts Avenue NE ☎ 202/371 9219), American Express (✉ 1150 Connecticut Avenue NW ☎ 202/457 1300) or at Ruesch International (✉ 825 14th Street NW ☎ 202/408 1200).

- Money transfer: you can send or receive a MoneyGram from American Express (☎ 800/926 9400) for up to $20,000. MoneyGram agents are in more than 70 countries. Western Union (☎ 800/325 6000) is linked to 22,000 locations in 78 countries.

Etiquette

- Washington is part of the South in many matters of courtesy. 'Please'

and 'thank-you' are not forgotten phrases and you should use them.

- Despite being a political city, Washington is basically rather informal. Some restaurants require a jacket and tie, but jeans and tennis shoes are acceptable in many others. For sightseeing and many other activities what is comfortable is OK.

Places of worship

- Episcopal (Anglican): National Cathedral ✉ Wisconsin and Massachusetts Avenues NW ☎ 202/537 6200)

- Jewish: Adas Israel ✉ Connecticut Avenue and Porter Street NW ☎ 202/362 4433

- Muslim: Islamic Mosque and Cultural Center ✉ 2551 Massachusetts Avenue NW ☎ 202/332 8343)

- Roman Catholic: National Shrine of the Immaculate Conception, ✉ Michigan Avenue and 4th Street NE ☎ 202/526 8300; Franciscan Monastery ✉ 14th and Quincy Streets NE ☎ 202/526 6800.

Toilets

- Finding restrooms (public toilets) can be difficult.

- There are facilities on the Mall around and west of the Washington Monument, as well as in all the museums.

- There are no public facilities in downtown or shopping areas.

- Fast food restaurants generally have restrooms, but you might have to ask for a key or a token to open the door.

Time differences

- Washington time is 5 hours behind the UK.

- For the current time ☎ 202/844 2525.

Electricity

- Electricity in the US is 110-120 volts at 60 Hz.
- You will need a converter to use 220-volt electric appliances.

PUBLIC TRANSPORT

- The subway (Metro) and bus (Metrobus) systems are run by the Washington Metropolitan Area Transit Authority (WMATA).
- Maps of the Metro system and some bus schedules are available in all Metro stations or at WMATA headquarters ✉ 600 5th Street NW.
- For general information or a copy of 'Welcome Aboard,' a helpful brochure ☎ 202/637 7000 daily from 6AM–11.30PM; for consumer assistance ☎ 202/637 1328; for transit police ☎ 202/962 2121.

The Metro

- The city's 20-year-old subway system, the Metro, is one of the cleanest and safest in the country.
- Trains run every few minutes, Mon–Fri 5:30AM–midnight, Sat and Sun 8AM–midnight.
- The basic fare ($1.10) goes up based on how far you are going and the time of day you are riding (fares are higher during rush hours, 5:30–9:30AM and 3–7PM). Maps in the stations tell you both the rush hour fare and regular fare to any destination station.
- You need a farecard to ride the Metro, both to enter and to exit. Farecard machines, located in the stations, take coins and $1, $5, $10 and $20 bills (the most change the machine will give you is about $5, so don't use a large bill if you are buying a low-value card).

- Insert your farecard into the slot on the side of the turnstile. Retrieve it once the gate opens as you will need it to exit. On exiting, insert the farecard into the turnstile. If your card is for the exact fare the gate will open and you can exit; if your card still has some money on it, it will again pop out the top of the turnstile. A red 'STOP' light means you need more money on your card to leave the station and must go the Addfare machine; insert your card and the machine will tell you how much additional fare is owed, pay that fare and return to the exit turnstile.
- The farecards are reusable until the card has a value of less than $1.10. Then, should you need another farecard, your old card can be used as cash in the farecard machine by putting it in the 'Used Farecard Trade-In' slot.
- A $5 one-day pass is available for unlimited trips at weekends, holidays or after 9:30AM weekdays. These passes are available at Metro Sales Outlets, including the Metro Center station and some hotels, banks and grocery stores.
- If you plan to transfer to a bus upon leaving the Metro, get a transfer before boarding your train from the dispenser located next to the escalator that goes down to the train level.

Buses

- The bus system covers a much wider area than does the Metro.
- The fare within the city is $1.10.
- Free bus-to-bus transfers are available from the driver and are good for about 2 hours at designated Metrobus transfer points.

Taxis

- Taxi fares are based on a somewhat hard-to-understand zone system. Maps showing the zones must be displayed in all cabs but even so it is still difficult to know when you are in which zone.
- The base fare for one passenger within a zone is $3.20, with a $1.25 charge for each extra passenger and a $1 surcharge Mon–Fri from 4 to 6.30PM.
- If you think you've been overcharged, get the driver's name and cab number and threaten to call the DC Taxicab Commission (☎ 202/645 6018).

Car rental

- Alamo (☎ 800/327 9633)
- Avis (☎ 800/331 1212, 800/879 2847 in Canada)
- Budget (☎ 800/527 0700)
- Dollar (☎ 800/800 4000)
- Hertz (☎ 800/654 3131, 800/263 0600 in Canada)
- National (☎ 800/227 7368)

MEDIA & COMMUNICATIONS

Telephones

- Local telephone calls (including nearby suburbs) cost 25 cents; insert your money, then dial your number.
- There are three local area codes: 202 (Washington), 301 (Maryland, except numbers in Baltimore which are prefixed by 410) and 703 (Virginia). Only use area code when dialling outside your own area.
- Directory enquiries (known as 'Information'): ☎ 411 (usually free).
- Police or medical emergency: ☎ 911.

Post offices

- The National Postal Museum (Massachusetts Avenue and North Capitol Street NE), next door to Union Station, is a working post office.
- Other branches include Farragut (✉ 1125 19th Street NW ☎ 202/523 2506), Georgetown (✉ 1215 31st Street NW ☎ 202/523 2405), L'Enfant Plaza (✉ 458 L'Enfant Plaza SW ☎ 202/523 2013) and Washington Square (✉ 1050 Connecticut Avenue NW ☎ 202/523 2631).
- The cost of mailing a postcard to the UK is 40 cents; the cost of sending a 1-ounce (28g) letter is 95 cents. The cost of mailing a letter within the US is 32 cents.

Newspapers

- Washington has two major daily newspapers, *The Washington Post* and the *Washington Times*.
- In addition, there are various neighbourhood weekly newspapers serving Capitol Hill, Georgetown, Adams-Morgan and other areas.
- The *City Paper*, a free weekly with an emphasis on entertainment, is available from newspaper boxes around town and at many restaurants, clubs and other outlets.
- The *Washington Blade*, a free weekly aimed at gays and lesbians, is available at many restaurants, bars and stores, especially in the Dupont Circle, Adams-Morgan and Capitol Hill areas, or at Lambda Rising (✉ 1625 Connecticut Avenue NW ☎ 202/462 6969) or Lammas (✉ 1426 21st Street NW ☎ 202/775–8218).
- *Washingtonian*, a monthly magazine, has a calendar of events, dining information,

articles about the city or prominent people here and also does many 'Best of' issues on topics such as restaurants or types of restaurants.

- *Where/Washington* is a free monthly magazine listing popular things to do. If your hotel doesn't have a copy ☎ 202/463 4550.

- Other national newspapers are available at newspaper boxes around the city.

International newsagents

- International newspapers and magazines are available at some news stores, including News World (✉ 1001 Connecticut Avenue NW ☎ 202/872 0190) and the Newsroom (✉ 1753 Connecticut Avenue NW ☎ 202/332 1489).

EMERGENCIES

Sensible precautions

- Washington's reputation as a dangerous city is somewhat unfair – it is approximately as safe as any medium to large city anywhere. Violent crime is mainly concentrated far from the downtown and tourist areas, in sections of the city you would not really have any cause to visit.

- Use the same precautions you would use in any city: at night or on quiet streets, always be aware of what's going on around you; if it is possible, walk with someone rather than walking alone; it is wise to use taxis for travelling to less populous areas at night.

- Should you be attacked, co-operate, then immediately call the police on 911.

Lost property

- Metro or Metrobus: ☎ 202/962 1195
- Smithsonian museums: ☎ 202/357 2700
- Other lost articles: check with the police at ☎ 202/727 1010.

Medical treatment

- Dial 911 for assistance.
- The hospital closest to downtown is George Washington University Hospital (✉ 901 23rd Street NW ☎ 202/994 3211, emergencies only).
- Prologue (☎ 202/362 8677) is a referral service that locates doctors, dentists and urgent-care clinics in the greater Washington area.
- The DC Dental Society (☎ 202/547 7615) operates a referral line weekdays 8–4.

Medicines

- Late-night pharmacies: CVS Pharmacy operates 24-hour pharmacies at 14th Street and Thomas Circle NW (☎ 202/628 0720) and at 7 Dupont Circle NW (☎ 202/785 1466).

Embassy and consulate

- If you lose your passport or need information on citizenship or other personal records, contact the consular section (✉ 19 Observatory Circle NW) of the British Embassy at 202/986 0205. If you don't hear the particular information you need on the list of options, call the chancery at the British Embassy (✉ 3100 Massachusetts Avenue NW) at 202/462 1340.

- All foreign embassies or consular headquarters are located in or around Washington. Consult the telephone book for address and telephone details of these offices.

INDEX

ACKNOWLEDGEMENTS

The Automobile Association would like to thank the following photographers, libraries and associations for their assistance in the preparation of this book: M GOSTELOW 7, 57; THE PHILLIPS COLLECTION 27; PICTURES COLOUR LIBRARY LTD 13a; SPECTRUM COLOUR LIBRARY 13b, 41b

All remaining pictures were taken by Ethel Davies and are held in the Association's own library (AA PHOTO LIBRARY).

Copy-editor: *Beth Ingpen*
Verifier: *Judy Sykes*
Indexer: *Marie Lorimer*
Original design: *Design FX*